# APOCALYPSE NOW

Wisps of smoke began trailing upward from several locations, including second-story windows. Then flames spurted out. Immediately caught by a brisk wind gusting up to thirty miles per hour, the fire scooted across the wood frame buildings in a rush. In moments, while horrified law enforcement officers watched helplessly, the compound erupted in a volcano of flame and smoke. . . .

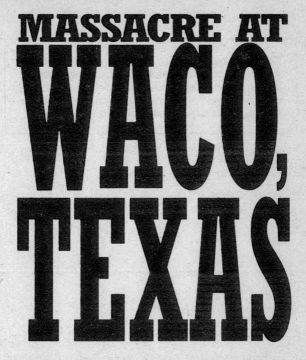

# MASSACRE AT WACO, TEXAS

**The Shocking Story of Cult Leader
David Koresh and the Branch Davidians**

# CLIFFORD L. LINEDECKER

ST. MARTIN'S PAPERBACKS

MASSACRE AT WACO, TEXAS

Copyright © 1993 by Clifford L. Linedecker.

Cover photograph by G. Reed Schumann/Reuter, courtesy of Bettmann.

ISBN: 0-312-95226-0

Printed in the United States of America

St. Martin's Paperbacks edition/July 1993

10 9 8 7 6 5 4 3 2 1

# Author's Note

The central figure in this story, Vernon Howell, legally changed his name in 1990 to David Koresh. In an effort to avoid confusion, throughout the book he is referred to by whichever name he was using at the time.

For my great-grandfather, Albert Drake, whom I never knew. He was a self-taught artist and mapmaker and an itinerant preacher from northern Indiana who walked to Kentucky to exhort against the evils of strong drink. Moonshiners nailed him inside his cabin and burned him to death. They thought he was a revenuer.

# Contents

# Introduction

AS AN AUTHOR AND FORMER JOURNALIST I've hobnobbed over the years with members of an eclectic assortment of religious sects and cults ranging from warmed-over 1960s hippies turned Sufi, to brooding Satanists, to pallid devotees of the Bhaktivedanta Swami Prabhupada who shaved their heads and dressed in saffron robes while chanting, "Hare Krishna."

But I've never forgotten the heavily bearded baseball players and the plain, pious women of the House of David.

I was just a couple of years or so into grade school when my parents and a favorite older cousin drove me on the forty-mile trip from my home in Plymouth, Indiana, to Benton Harbor, Michigan.

Fifty years ago the House of David settlement at Benton Harbor was still a thriving community. Although at the time I was more interested in its miniature train rides and popcorn, I couldn't help but be impressed by the preserved corpse of the long-dead founder of the cult, who was still on display there in a glass-topped casket, patiently awaiting resurrection. An itinerant preacher, Benjamin Purnell never learned to read or write. Nevertheless, his rhetorical genius, manipulative cant, and ability to twist and mold the biblical prophecies of the Book of Revelation to his own benefit enabled him to found a community of hundreds of devout followers while building a personal fortune for himself.

Purnell lured his recruits and assured their loyalty by convincing them they would be among the 144,000 faithful souls selected to rule with the returned Messiah in God's Kingdom on Earth during the millenium ushered in by the final world's-end struggle between good and evil. Today, many Christian fundamentalists talk of the moment when the 144,000 elite are borne away to heaven as the Rapture.

A few years ago after a television appearance in Virginia promoting one of my books, a sincere young Christian was driving me to the airport at breakneck speed and talking enthusiastically about the anticipated event. When the Rapture occurs, he explained, the 144,000 will be swept to paradise in the flicker of an eye. "I'll be gone, and you'll still be here," he said, glancing at me in the passenger seat with a look of smug superiority.

It was a sobering thought. I never expected to be among the 144,000 anyway, but we were running late for my flight and passing cars and trucks as if they were standing still. I didn't want the driver vanishing and leaving me alone in the passenger seat to deal with some eighteen-wheeler at the next stoplight.

There weren't any tractor-trailer trucks around in 1903 when Purnell established the House of David in Benton Harbor. He rode in buggies and on ocean liners during his travels to seek out converts from most of the English-speaking world. The lives of his flock were devoted to work and prayer, and their property and money were turned over to their leader.

Although he taught his followers that strict celibacy was the path to spiritual salvation, Purnell made different rules for himself and preyed on all of the best-looking females. He was a shameless sexual satyr, but his disgraceful behavior was tolerated by his obedient followers because they believed he was Christ returned. Like the Shakers of Mother Ann Lee who made such beautiful functional furniture but no babies, after the death of the House of David's charismatic leader the supply of converts dwindled until the religious community eventually died out.

I dredged up some of my memories of the House of David a few months ago after my editor, Charles Spicer, telephoned and asked how I would like to catch a flight to Waco, Texas. There was no reason to ask why, and I hurried to Waco. We both knew there had been a tragic shootout there between agents of the Bureau of Alcohol, Tobacco, and Firearms and heavily armed members of a clannish religious commune known as Branch Davidians. Four ATF agents had been shot to death and an unknown number of people inside the compound killed and injured.

When I got to central Texas and began looking into the religious convictions and activities of the cultists I was struck by the dramatic parallel between the barricaded Branch Davidians and the House of David I remembered in Benton Harbor.

Both Branch Davidian leader David Koresh and Purnell reportedly made similar claims of being the Messiah returned to lead the elite faithful into the Apocalypse and the millennium. Both had recruited heavily in England and Australia as well as in the United States. And like Purnell, Koresh took the most attractive women among his followers for his own. He even set up his own harem. He called it the House of David.

It's difficult for most people who have never been captive to a cult to understand how intelligent, loving, and devout men and women could buy such an outrageous line of claptrap and totally turn over their lives to a David Koresh.

But he apparently accomplished the masterful sales job the same way Purnell did: by convincing his flock that sacrifice now would assure them of a heavenly reward later as members of the Lord's elite 144,000.

I was thinking about that while I stood with a horde of news reporters and photographers along a farm road a few miles from the sprawl of two-story buildings where Koresh and a hundred or so of his followers were holed up. The barricaded cultists were surrounded by an army of law enforcement officers. But for the moment, Koresh was holding most of the face cards. And he insisted that he and his people, who included many children, weren't coming out until God told him it was okay.

Members of the FBI negotiating team and

other agencies and individuals were at a distinct disadvantage attempting to reason with someone who talked in surrealistic biblical cant and insisted he was in direct communion with God.

Unsurprisingly then, there was a pervasive feeling of helplessness among many of those witnessing the siege. In many ways it reminded me of riding in the passenger seat of a speeding car and suddenly noticing, with a sick feeling in my stomach, that the driver had vanished. It was almost like heading for an eighteen-wheeler at ninety miles an hour with nobody at the controls.

Clifford L. Linedecker
Lantana, Florida
May 1993

# Prologue

DOZENS OF HOLLYWOOD HORSE OPERAS have made the central Texas city of Waco almost synonymous with the Wild West for generations of movie and television fans. Either brash young guns adopted Waco as their nickname, or story lines were set amid the former dirt streets of the dusty cowboy town. There was good reason for that.

During Waco's early years the behavior of many of its citizens and casual visitors was wild and woolly. The town developed a reputation almost from its beginnings for being ruled by the gun.

Waco is located on a fertile stretch of Texas plains land fed by the Brazos and Bosque rivers, amid rich farmland that through the years has supported thriving agribusinesses in cotton, corn, and other crops. But it wasn't farmers who were responsible for the town's violent reputation. It was the rambunctious cowpokes, gamblers, and gunslingers moving along the Chisholm Trail, some passing through, some lingering, some dying violently, who left the romantic flavor of the Wild West on the city.

Shootouts were so common in the streets, saloons, and whorehouses that stagecoach drivers called the rowdy cowboy town "Six-Shooter Junction." Guns have always played an important role in the community.

In 1898 William Cowper Brand, a sharp-tongued editor who wouldn't tolerate narrow-minded religious hypocrites, died in a gun battle after he picked a fight in his internationally known weekly newspaper, the *Iconoclast*, with the Baptists at Baylor University. One of his most vitriolic attacks came in a story he penned about a pretty Brazilian maid who had mysteriously become pregnant while working for the president of the university. Brand sarcastically described her baby as a beautiful "three-pound

Baylor diploma." Shortly after that the feisty editor was bushwhacked by the angry father of a Baylor coed and shot in the back, but he turned and killed his attacker before he died.

Frontier law was already being ruled by the gun more than half a century earlier when in 1837 the famous Texas Rangers established their first fort along the Brazos River near an Indian village. The Rangers faced off with Cherokee and Comanche Indian warriors in their fight to open the valley for white settlement. A weaker tribe of Huacos (pronounced Wacos) had been run off by the stronger, more fierce Indians a few years earlier.

The daring feats of the Rangers soon became a good yardstick against which to measure the worth of other hard-riding, hard-shooting lawmen whose stamina and courage helped tame the Wild West.

The old-time lawmen and their professional descendants are memorialized in Waco by the Texas Ranger Hall of Fame and Museum at Fort Fisher. Company F of the Rangers is still headquartered there, as well.

Despite the police presence, however, some citizens of Waco and outlying areas of McLennan County, like those of other American communities, still settle problems with six-shooters and other handguns. And many residents are dismayed at Waco's headline-grabbing link with two of the most notorious killers in recent Texas history.

One of those killers is David Wayne Spence, who is on death row at the Texas State Penitentiary in Huntsville after carrying out a savage murder that went terribly awry. Spence is awaiting execution by lethal injection for the rape-murder of two teenage girls and the slaying of their male companion. The bodies of the victims were dumped along the shores of Lake Waco after the 1982 slayings.

Ten years later, Kenneth "Mad Dog" McDuff was charged with the murders of a clerk abducted from a Quik-Pac convenience store in Waco and another young woman from nearby Bryan. McDuff, who police said was a suspect in the slayings of several other Texas women, was previously condemned to death for slaying one of a trio of teenagers killed near Fort Worth in 1966. But his sentence was later commuted to life in prison after the U. S. Supreme Court temporarily struck down death penalty laws. In 1989 he was paroled during a period when corrections authorities were being pressured to relieve prison overcrowding. By early 1993 he was behind bars again, once more convicted of murder, this time for the kidnap slaying of the clerk, Melissa Ann Northrup.

Even earlier, in the 1980s, Henry Lee Lucas, a one-eyed bisexual with killing ways and a vivid imagination, admitted to committing more than 360 murders while drifting through thirty-six states. Three of the killings occurred in McLennan County, he said. Lucas later recanted most of his confessions, but he is still on death row in the prison at Huntsville.

Waco has experienced other troubles and public relations disappointments as well. Legalized whorehouses weren't shut down in the city until the World War I years. And for a time, a half-century ago or more, it was a stronghold of the Ku Klux Klan. In 1953 a devastating tornado roared through the downtown area, killing 114 people and destroying more than three hundred buildings. And early in 1993 a report issued by the Greater Washington Research Center in the nation's capital listed six Texas cities among the twenty communities with the worst poverty rates in the United States. Waco was number 18.

Community leaders would prefer their city of 104,000 be recognized for its fourteen museums, Madison Cooper Airport, a fine zoo, excellent universities and colleges, and the strong mainstream Protestant Christian ethic. Located along Interstate 35 about midway between the metropolitan sprawl of Dallas–Fort Worth and the state's capital city of Austin, Waco built so many churches, and in some ways its image became so puritanical, that people sometimes call it by yet another nickname—Jerusalem on the Brazos.

The Dr Pepper Museum, commemorating the fountain drink refined more than a century ago by a local beverage chemist, R. S. Lazenby, is one of Waco's most popular tourist stops. The drink was originally mixed in the Old Corner Drug Store, and Lazenby fiddled with the concoction for two years before developing the ultimate formula in 1885.

But Waco is also home to the Texas State Technical Institute, Paul Quinn College, the McLennan Community College, and to Baylor University, a 148-year-old Baptist school that is known for its scholarship as well as its outstanding football team. Longtime McLennan County Sheriff Jack Harwell earned his degree in criminal justice there.

Baylor is so conservative that a few years ago, when a *Playboy* magazine photographer showed up in town to snap pictures of coeds for a feature titled "Women of the Southwest Conference," the university president threatened to expel any students who posed. One senior student wound up barred from the graduation ceremony as a result of the flap.

It wasn't until early in 1993 that university officials announced that a nude figure drawing class would finally be permitted for its art students, beginning with the fall semester. But male models were instructed that they must wear athletic supporters. Even then members of the Baptist General Convention of Texas prayed and pleaded with the university to reconsider its decision, and a few days after the controversy began they were rewarded. The school, which had broken its strong ties with the convention a couple of years earlier, reinstituted the ban. And Baylor still doesn't allow on-campus dancing.

But attitudes on campus, as they are in most of the rest of Waco and throughout Texas, are more liberal when it comes to guns. Like twenty-three other states early in 1993, Texas had no gun registration laws. And Texans could become legal gun dealers by paying thirty dollars to the U.S. Bureau of Alcohol, Tobacco, and Firearms for a federal permit. So it's perhaps unsurprising that there are more licensed gun dealers in the Lone Star State than obstetricians. It's easier and cheaper to sell guns than it is to deliver babies.

In 1991, the most recent year for which statistics are available, Texas had the dubious distinction of being the only state where more people were killed by guns than in traffic accidents. More than 16,500 residents, including police officers, owned machine guns. According to law enforcement authorities and other sources, some seventeen million people in the state own sixty million firearms. That averages out to about four guns per person.

Early in 1993 a disturbing number of those firearms belonged to a group of men, women, and children who lived together in a radical religious commune about ten miles east of Waco. The arms arsenal was believed to include Ruger mini-14 rifles capable of firing 40 rounds per minute if semiautomatic and 750 rounds per minute if automatic, AK-47 assault rifles capable of firing 600 rounds per minute, Israeli submachine guns, AR-15 semiautomatic rifles, .223-caliber semiautomatic rifles, Beretta semiautomatic pistols with fifteen-shot magazines, 9-mm Glock handguns, a .50-caliber machine gun, and hand grenades. It was an astonishing array of firepower.

Residents of the heavily fortified compound called themselves Branch Davidians. And they were waiting, along with their charismatic leader, for the Apocalypse.

# CHAPTER ONE

# Bloody Sunday

*We're talking about Waco! If someone comes in your house blazing away, cops or whoever they are, you're gonna do some shootin back.*

—*Pickup truck driver*

IT WAS ABOUT SIX-THIRTY ON A CHILL, drizzly late winter Sunday morning, and a thick ground fog hung heavy over the stubble and scrub-brush flatland around the the L-shaped Branch Davidian compound when thirty-three-year-old Paul G. Fatta and his fourteen-year-old son, Kalani, pulled away in a truck. It was an approximate two-hour drive nearly due south along Interstate 35 to Austin, where Fatah planned to sell some guns, and he wanted to get there early.

The father and son were on their way to the Austin Coliseum to attend the Original Austin Gun Show, a two-times-a-year affair that draws sportsmen, collectors, and other gun enthusiasts from throughout much of central Texas.

Fatta was a regular at gun shows in Austin, Dallas, Fort Worth, San Antonio, and other cities in Texas and sold everything from camouflage clothing to military-type ready-to-eat meals, gun grips, and weapons.

Back at Mount Carmel nearly everyone among the more than one hundred men, women, and children who lived there had already been up for an hour and they were busy with their normal morning chores and routine.

Although the day long prayers of the Saturday Sabbath were behind them, members of the strict religious community arose early for more prayer, Bible study, and hard work. The devotions and honest labor were the focus of every day they spent together.

Women assigned to kitchen duties that day barely had time to wash and dress before they began preparing the sparse morning meal. Other women walked outside through the chill drizzle to pump water and fill a cistern that had pipes leading into the kitchen, or they carried the body waste collected overnight outside to dispose of it. And some busied themselves feeding the chickens, geese, and pets.

Several bony men shuffled outside to begin calisthenics and to run the obstacle course that had been personally designed by their leader. After their exercise they filed back into the large dining hall and sat down at long, plain wooden tables for a meager breakfast of fruit, bread, and milk or water. Later, after the work in the kitchen was done and the children settled, the women took their turn running or jogging around the track. While they ran they counted cadence and shouted out rhymes, military style, just as if they were marines. Koresh wanted his followers to be fit, healthy, and strong.

There was always plenty of work to do for members of the commune who didn't leave for outside jobs or other activities after the exercise. Except for the dreariest winter months, the cultists planted and cared for a string of vegetable gardens around the compound. The homegrown crops were then used for vegetarian stews, salads, and other plain meals prepared by the women.

Buildings were linked to each other by above-ground entrances and passageways, as well as by a series of cement tunnels that snaked underground, and they required regular painting and other maintenance. A new swimming pool was currently being constructed, and a gym was already completed, although it was being used for storage.

The Branch Davidians called on professional builders and craftsmen only when they absolutely had to because it was work they didn't know how to do themselves. Even when they did break down and brought in skilled help they skimped on materials and insisted the job be done as cheaply as possible.

Older children were kept busy with prayer or with the Bible study that occupied much of their time when they weren't being taught the three Rs or attending to other lessons.

Their normal schedule called for Bible study for an hour beginning at nine in the morning and again at three in the afternoon. But they couldn't always count on getting off so easy. When the Prophet himself conducted the studies, he sometimes harangued them for eight hours or more, occasionally as long as sixteen hours at a stretch. And they had better pay strict attention.

There wasn't much time lately in their carefully regimented lives for fussing over the new puppies an Alsatian bitch had given birth to a couple of days earlier.

But on Sunday, February 28, even the Prophet was up and moving around, and that was unusual. David Koresh, the Branch Davidians' dimpled, long-haired, charismatic young leader, set different rules for himself than he did for his devout followers. Although the others were expected to be up before dawn, he customarily lingered in bed until two or three o'clock in the afternoon. He lounged in his private quarters, where the walls were hung with posters promoting the heavy-metal band Megadeath and rocker Ted Nugent, watching MTV or other television shows. He especially liked Madonna and confided to his followers that someday she would be his wife. He could watch and listen to her scream and prance around a stage for hours.

Then he would stay up until midnight or later, talking Scriptures or tossing down a few beers while strumming his guitar and belting out his own noisy rock compositions. Everyone else was forced to remain awake until he finally tired and they were at last permitted to drop exhausted into their beds for a few hours' sleep.

Only Koresh's personal apartment was equipped with a television set, a radio, stereo, other electronic equipment, heat, and air-conditioning. There were none of those amenities in the dormitories for his followers. No one else was allowed to have a beer or other alcoholic drink anytime he wished. And he was the only man permitted to wear his hair long, shoulder length. Koresh never served in the military, but somehow he had learned the old saw that "Rank has its privileges."

Buildings in the seventy-seven-acre compound, which was about the size of an average city block, had no central heating and almost no indoor plumbing. Only a trailer occupied by several of the older cult members a few miles from Mount Carmel had flush toilets and central heat.

Despite the apparent routine nature of the Sunday morning activities, however, most of the adults at Mount Carmel either knew or seemed to suspect that they weren't beginning simply another typical day. Koresh and his followers were worried and edgy. Defectors had dropped out, then turned on their former leader, and were spreading stories about a harem of wives, child abuse, a huge stockpile of weapons, and plans to unleash some kind of a crazed miniwar on Waco. A private detective hired by dropouts in Australia had been snooping around Waco for months asking questions and talking with local police.

On Saturday, the Davidian Sabbath, the *Waco Tribune-Herald* had begun publishing a seven-part copyrighted series of articles, "The Sinful Messiah," about Koresh and his followers that had taken more than eight months and scores of interviews to put together. The first article in the series talked of court records and disaffected members reputedly accusing Koresh of being a polygamist, having sex with underage girls, and otherwise abusing children.

The compound had indeed been turned into a fortress and an arsenal. A couple of boxes of hand grenades sat on a table in the dining room. Douglas Wayne Martin, a forty-two-year-old Harvard-educated lawyer from the borough of Queens in New York City, was puttering around with a string of grenades around his neck. Elsewhere in the compound, huge boxes of ammunition for a bewildering array of high-powered semiautomatic weapons were stacked against the wall. And nearly three hundred guns, many of them military-style assault rifles, were stacked in an armory.

Nevertheless, when a man the Davidians knew as Richard Gonzales drove up to the compound, he was welcomed inside. A few days earlier, Gonzales and several other young men had rented a ramshackle house across a field about 260 yards from Mount Carmel. They said they were college students. After Gonzales showed interest in the Davidians' religious philosophy, he was permitted to share in several hours of Bible study. The well-spoken young man was also given a Cook's tour of the compound.

Gonzales appeared to be impressed and developed a habit of dropping by for more lessons and discussion of the Scriptures when he had an opportunity. The Branch Davidians continued to share the Scriptures with him, but they weren't completely comfortable when he was around. He and his friends seemed to be a trifle old for college students, they had too much money to spend, their cars were too new, and they never turned their lights on at night.

There were other reasons for the suspicions and discomfort of the cultists. A few months earlier, friendly neighbors had tipped them off that police had asked permission to install recording devices on their property. The lawmen said they wanted to find out if Koresh and his people were firing illegal automatic weapons.

Koresh had responded to the news by summoning a couple of his most trusted male followers, called "Mighty Men," who were permitted to carry guns and were responsible for protection of the commune and its occupants. Koresh and the Mighty Men drove to the McLennan County sheriff's office in Waco. There they confronted Lieutenant Gene Barber about the matter. Barber, it was later claimed, had assured them that the law was satisfied the guns kept at the compound were legal.

Tension had remained high at the compound, however. Koresh's preaching and biblical discussions were becoming increasingly paranoid and egocentric. He warned of a bloody confrontation with authorities and returned time and again to ominous predictions that the Apocalypse and Armageddon were rapidly approaching.

Armed guards were stationed at the entrance to the compound and patrolled the grounds at night. Others were posted around the clock on top of the ugly square four-story watchtower. It was the tallest building at Mount Carmel and provided a 360-degree view of the compound. Koresh's followers had improved the fortifications by stacking cinder blocks along several of the outer walls.

Both men and women were expected to take their turns at guard duty. And both sexes were required to practice firing M-16 rifles and to train with other firearms from the arsenal.

As the self-professed Prophet, or Anointed One, Koresh enforced strict discipline and demanded complete obedience from his followers. And although he would later deny it, he was quoted in the *Tribune-Herald* as declaring: "If the Bible is true, then I'm Christ." And David Koresh was a man with a firm belief in the Bible. But being Christ, he reputedly claimed, was no big deal.

Koresh's belief in the proximity of the End Times was so intense, in fact, that his followers had begun openly referring to the compound as Ranch Apocalypse. During the Christmas–New

Year holiday period, Perry Jones, an older member of the cult, had stopped in at Central Rental in Waco to pay a bill and had said that Mount Carmel had a new name. He said it was called Ranch Apocalypse, and that members of the commune were cleaning it up and working to make it a nicer place to live.

Some outsiders might have considered the name Mount Carmel to be sinister enough without the change. The name can be found in 1 Kings 18 of the Old Testament and refers to the struggle between Elijah and pagan prophets that led to the death of the pagans.

So there should have been no surprise that strangers like Gonzales were closely watched. Some of the Branch Davidians were openly suspicious of their inquisitive neighbor and carefully guarded their conversation around him.

Shortly after Gonzales's arrival Sunday morning, one of the men in the main building called Koresh away. There had been a telephone call, and another resident of the compound had just arrived with a message as well.

When Koresh returned to the room and walked toward the visitor, he was quoting Scriptures and had a disturbing message. He said the federal Bureau of Alcohol, Tobacco, and Firearms and the Texas National Guard were coming to get him.

"Neither ATF or the National Guard will ever get me. They got me once, and they will never get me again," he vowed. "They are coming: the time has come."

Alarmed, Gonzales told the cult leader he hadn't eaten yet that morning, and was going out for breakfast. The visitor hurried away. Branch Davidians watched from windows as he cut through the pastures, heading for the house he and his pals had rented.

Heavy gray clouds obscured any possible light from the moon or stars when the small army of rugged men and women began to drift out of their motel rooms in Waco before dawn. Dressed in military-style fatigues, camouflage greens, and blue jumpsuits with deep flapped pockets for ammunition clips, flak jackets, combat boots, helmets, and caps, they headed for a staging area, where they assembled near a convoy of vehicles. Their jackets and shirts were imprinted with the words ATF AGENTS in large yellow-and-white block letters. The logos identified them as agents of the federal Bureau of Alcohol, Tobacco, and Firearms.

The agents were armed with a formidable collection of firearms including Smith & Wesson .357s, Smith & Wesson .38s, 9-mm semiautomatic pistols, Remington 870 pump-action 12-

gauge shotguns, Ruger mini-14 semiautomatic rifles, Winchester 70 sniper rifles, and Heckler & Koch submachine guns.

They had been assembling in Waco for days, traveling from the ATF's Dallas, Houston, and New Orleans field divisions and from the Fort Hood Army Base. Two U.S. marshals from the Waco office accompanied the raiding team and were prepared to take custody of prisoners. A command post was set up on the campus of the Texas State Technical Institute in Waco for senior officers to coordinate the operation.

Some of the men peered curiously at vending machines holding copies of the Sunday newspaper, featuring the second segment of the series about "The Sinful Messiah" on the front page. But the only vending machines most of them had time for delivered black coffee, and several of the agents were still sipping at steaming Styrofoam cups when they began scrambling into a pair of cattle trailers. There was barely time for them to arrange their weapons before they were covered with green tarpaulins. A few minutes later the trailers, pulled by pickup trucks and escorted by a convoy of plain cars and vans, moved out of the parking lots. The convoy headed east out of the city and onto a stretch of asphalt-paved Farm Road 2491 headed toward Mount Carmel.

The ATF's own investigators and other sources had determined that the cultists had stockpiled an arsenal of powerful weapons worth nearly two hundred thousand dollars and believed to include scores of illegal machine guns and huge stores of explosives. Attorneys had filed affidavits in support of search and arrest warrants, alleging various violations of federal firearms laws.

The cultists were accused of illegally converting semiautomatic weapons to automatics for rapid fire, of amassing stocks of gunpowder, ammunition, hand grenades, chemicals that could be used in the manufacture of explosives, and other arms and equipment, including a starlight filter like those used by soldiers in Vietnam to help pick out targets in the dark.

Other offenses, including the physical and sexual abuse of children, were also suspected, and cited in affidavits filed in support of the February warrants and in later court documents. Federal agents had also heard stories that the cultists were manufacturing their own illegal silencers and tinkering with model airplanes capable of delivering explosive charges and becoming flying bombs.

ATF operatives had been checking out the cultists for more than a year after picking up various tidbits of information indicating the Branch Davidians were stockpiling weapons. But the investigation didn't move into high gear until mid-summer, after executives with the United Parcel Service reported that a package addressed to the Branch Davidians had broken open and revealed that components for hand grenades were inside.

Police in Waco were first notified of the discovery, but the probe was quickly taken over by the ATF. The empty grenade casings, which had neither charges inside nor firing pins, were inspected by investigators. Then at their instructions the box was resealed and the material was delivered to the compound.

Subsequent investigation indicated that chemicals, gunpowder, and other components were being purchased by the cultists to manufacture explosives or explosive devices. Furthermore, eight thousand pounds of ammunition, 260 ammunition magazines, and enough parts to enable the assembling of hundreds of semi-automatic and automatic weapons were believed to have been added to the arsenal at the compound.

Now, nearly eight months after the accidental discovery the previous July, ATF agents were on their way to serve search and arrest warrants and to seize the armaments.

Sunday morning during the group's first scheduled prayer service of the day was considered the best and safest time to launch the raid because the men would be separated from the women and children. Also, presumably, they wouldn't have the stockpiled weapons ready at hand.

Several civilian vehicles, including unmarked cars with a reporter and photographer for the *Tribune-Herald*, along with twenty-nine-year-old John McLemore and a cameraman from Waco's KWTX-TV, were already parked along Farm Road 2491 about a quarter of a mile from the commune. Someone had tipped them off about the planned raid. They had been waiting since about 7:00 A.M., watching the dirt road leading to the scatter of flimsy beige one- and two-story buildings in the complex while the orange midwinter Texas sun pushed streaks of weak light through the depressing cloud cover.

An indolent herd of Holstein and Guernsey cows grazed placidly in a nearby field while the journalists watched the convoy approach. The rotors of a Texas National Guard Sikorsky Blackhawk helicopter rattled overhead as the chopper appeared a few hundred yards from the compound. A few minutes later two more National Guard Apache helicopters took up positions over the compound.

McLennan County residents with radio scanners puzzled over scraps of information picked up from walkie-talkies being used by the assault team as they pulled into the compound. Media reporters and photographers trailed after them in their own vehicles.

It was 9:55 A.M., the last day of February 1993, when an ATF agent pushed past the scatter of go-carts and Harley-Davidson motorcycles in front of the compound and pounded at the front door of the commune's main building. Behind him other agents were already leaping out of their trucks and cars and advancing on the compound in squads. Members of three entry teams spread out and hurried forward, with their weapons cocked and ready.

The plan had been put together with military precision by experienced senior agents and approved at the highest levels. The lightning assault was to be the culmination of eight months of intensive investigation and training. The raid was approved by Stephen E. Higgins in Washington, and other senior ATF officials. Higgins was a former frontline agent who was a career ATF man and the bureau's director since 1983.

The agents had trained secretly for the raid at Fort Hood, where buildings were set up to resemble those at the cult compound. Fort Hood, less than an hour's drive from Waco along I-35 and U.S. 190, sits at the edge of Killeen, Texas, where in October of 1991 a berserk loner who hated women shot to death twenty-three people and wounded nineteen at a crowded Luby's Cafeteria before dashing into a bathroom and killing himself. Thirty-five-year-old George Hennard crashed his pickup truck through a plate-glass window as people were eating lunch and began shooting them down with a brace of semiautomatic pistols. It was the worst mass murder in American history.

The ATF was to call on some of the same techniques that had made Hennard so successful. The strength of their scheme was to be its surprise, speed, simplicity, and overwhelming force.

A special team was assigned to take control of the arsenal next to Koresh's personal quarters; another team was to cut off and protect the women and children, while blocking the adult females from the gun room; and it was the job of the third squad to neutralize and capture Koresh and his adult male followers.

According to the strategy worked out by the experts, the first entry team was to be inside the front door within seven seconds after the convoy pulled up to the compound. All the assault teams would be deployed within thirteen seconds.

And within twenty-two seconds, a team would have scaled aluminum ladders, climbed into a second-story window, and been on the way to a room pinpointed by undercover agents and other informants as the cult's main armory. The locked room was believed to be filled with rows of neatly stacked military-type assault weapons and thousands of rounds of ammunition. In most ways the plan was very similar to the type of carefully orchestrated assaults the ATF had used successfully before.

A cultist peered out of the opened double doors to the main building. It was Koresh. He was dressed all in black and appeared to be un-armed.

"Federal agents with a search warrant!" the ATF man growled.

Koresh lurched backward and slammed the doors shut.

ATF raiders began yelling, "Come out! Come out!"

Then all hell broke loose.

A sheet of gunfire erupted. Shots were sprayed from the house, dormitories, garages, farm buildings, and guard tower in the complex. The deadly spray was so fierce that for a moment some of the agents thought the bullets were being fired *into* the compound. Then, as the deadly whisper of flying metal enveloped them and their companions began to drop, they real-ized the hail of gunfire was coming through the windows and walls—at them.

The question of who began shooting first

would eventually become a matter of bitter debate, but the law officers and the barricaded cultists had no time then to worry about such things. They were facing off in a furious firefight.

Ted Royster, special agent in charge of the ATF Dallas office, was in one of the helicopters overhead, and it was fired on and struck almost instantaneously as the shootout began on the ground. Another chopper was also hit, but the gunfire failed to bring either of the aircraft down. An officer in one of the helicopters was videotaping the action.

Two of the three agents assigned to secure the weapons cache spurted through the second-floor window and had started toward the basement vault when the walls around them exploded. Cultists were firing through the walls from other rooms, creating a firestorm of deadly wood and metal splinters. A couple of members of the team crashed back outside through the window and were dragged away by colleagues to sheltered areas behind vehicles and trees.

Robert J. "Robb" Williams, the third member of the special team, dropped when he was hit in the shoulder by a bullet that apparently came from the watchtower. A moment later he was on his feet again, protecting his teammates with cover fire, when another bullet slammed through his helmet, killing him.

Agent Steve Willis was just beginning his dash from the stopped vehicles when a bullet struck him in the head. Other agents screamed and rolled to the ground when they were hit by shrapnel from hand grenades tossed by cultists.

Cartridges fired from high-velocity rifles tore through the metal doors of cars and trucks, shattered bones, and ripped through flesh. A woman agent yelled in alarm and pain when she was shot in the hand.

Forty-six-year-old J. William Buford, a decorated veteran of Vietnam who heads the agency's Little Rock, Arkansas, office, was on a roof when he crumpled with a shot in the left hip. Then another slammed into his thigh, but he managed to roll off the roof, breaking four ribs when he landed. He was pinned down by the heavy fusillade, and another bullet creased his nose before a heroic agent used his own body to protect his wounded colleague.

Meanwhile, emergency medical technicians who had accompanied the tactical teams scurried through the heavy gunfire to the side of the injured. The medics kept their backs bent protectively to lower their silhouettes. From somewhere within the compound, agents heard the clatter of a heavy weapon that sounded like a .50-caliber heavy machine gun. Fifty-calibers are devastating weapons that can be used to shoot down airplanes; they spray armor-piercing metal slugs the size of small carrots.

Some of the cultists crouched on rooftops or firing from windows and doors were wearing ski masks, hoods, and black pajama outfits like those the Vietcong used during the war in Vietnam.

Twenty-nine-year-old Special Agent John T. Risenhoover from the agency's San Antonio office, a member of a special maneuvers team, was slammed backward as the wind was knocked out of him by four bullets that struck him in the chest. Three others hit him in an ankle, the right leg, and his hip. A bulletproof vest saved his life, but he was left writhing in agony. Other agents were dropping around him with a storm of fierce injuries inflicted by the blur of gunshots and grenades.

Kenneth M. King, an agent attached to the New Orleans ATF office, also rolled off a roof after he was hit. King was stretched out on the ground, yelling into his hand-held radio: "Somebody help me." He was shot six times. Most of the bullets struck him after he fell, and at least one high-velocity round pierced his body armor and slammed into his chest.

About three hundred yards away along the perimeter of the action, news reporters and photographers crouched behind their cars and trucks as bullets whistled through the air and smashed into the parked media vehicles and scrub trees around them. The right front tire of a Chevrolet Cavalier driven to the area by *Tribune-Herald* reporter Mark England exploded when it was hit by a bullet. Bullets also smashed into the car of the newspaper's photographer, Ray Aydelotte. The journalists abandoned both vehicles.

While hand grenades exploded among the assault team with bone-jarring thumps, and bullets continued flying past him, blowing out windshields and tires on cars and trucks, KWTX cameraman Dan Mulloney, forty-three-years old, began worrying that he might not see his two daughters again, and he hunkered down even closer to the ground.

ATF agents attempted to shoo the television men away from the scene. They weren't trained for firefights and they were tempting targets, but the newsmen didn't leave.

The surprise attack had backfired on the ATF, and it was they, not the cultists, who were taken off guard. Furthermore, the agents had to cope with other disadvantages during the fierce firefight they suddenly found themselves engaged in. There was trouble with their communication system, the hand-held phones and radios.

And it also appeared that the barricaded religious zealots had superior weapons. Moveover, the assault team was governed by stringent rules of police procedure, and there could be no firing through walls at noises or through cracked open doors at slashes of movement. As law officers, ATF agents were trained not to trigger their weapons unless they had clearly defined targets in their sights.

Nevertheless, the raiders fought fiercely, tossing concussion grenades that were loud and distracting although not lethal, and returning the fire of the armed cultists inside and on top of the buildings. It was hellish inside the structures. Women screamed and children scooted under beds, where they moaned and huddled in terror as gunfire clattered around them and bullets chewed huge chunks out of furniture and walls. Rooms and passageways were filled with blue smoke, needle-sharp wood splinters, and screams.

Koresh was just inside the closed front door when bullets shattered the wood and he was struck in the side. He lurched into another room. He was hit again, this time in a hand.

Forty-one-year-old Judy Schneider, the legal wife of Koresh's top lieutenant, Steven Schneider, and a member of the cult leader's personal harem, went down with a bullet in her shoulder. Another bullet ripped into her right hand. The

Alsatian bitch and another dog were killed when they were struck by bullets.

Thirty-five-year-old Scott Kojiro Sonobe stumbled and fell with a gunshot wound in his right thigh.

ATF snipers firing from the house rented by "Gonzales" and his friends were plucking off armed cultists. A skinny man in blue jeans, plaid shirt, and cowboy boots dropped his semiautomatic rifle and tumbled from the guard tower. Twenty-one-year-old Peter Gent, a Branch Davidian from Melbourne, Australia, was apparently dead when his body landed in brush just outside the compound. His twin sister, Nicole, and her three-year-old son, Dayland, were inside one of the buildings.

But the ATF had suffered devastating casualties with the first clatter of gunfire, and they were outgunned. They pulled back to safer positions a few hundred yards from the buildings, and an ATF agent yelled at McLemore, the television reporter, who was crouched nearby: "Hey, TV man, call for an ambulance!"

McLemore broke from his cover and sprinted several yards across an open space toward his truck. Ripping the door open, he slid into the seat and began radioing for help as bullets pinged off the vehicle's side.

Approximately forty-five minutes into the firefight, a senior agent in the house the undercover agents had rented got through by telephone to the compound and arranged a cease-fire. Shortly before noon a truce was agreed upon to permit the ATF to evacuate their dead and injured.

Nearly twenty agents were dead or wounded. An unknown number of cultists were also killed and many were injured, including the thirty-three-year-old leader. Koresh was alive, but police had no idea and no immediate means of determining how serious his injuries were.

The first concern of the government agents was keeping the uneasy truce alive and getting help for the injured agents. EMTs and ATF agents began loading the injured into waiting CareFlite helicopters, ambulances, pickup trucks, vans, and cars for the dash to hospitals in Waco.

McLemore and Mulloney joined healthy ATF men in lifting moaning officers, including one with an injured leg and another with a back injury, into the TV station's van. Then they lurched away from the fire zone with yet another agent folded over the hood who had a chest wound. Others perched precariously on the sides of the van, holding on through rolled-down windows. Some injured agents were given CPR by their colleagues during the twelve-mile trip by the fleet of makeshift emergency vehicles.

When the casualties began flooding into the emergency room, doctors at the Hillcrest Baptist Medical Center were waiting, as prepared as they could be under the circumstances. Local law officers and security guards had been picking up bits and pieces of information by police radio since the gunfight broke out at the compound, and they had passed the news on to the medical professionals at the hospital. The doctors and nurses had realized they were in for a bad day, and administrators had called in extra help.

It was a few minutes past noon when the casualties began coming in. The most critically injured arrived first. The ATF man shot in the head as he sprinted from the truck, and several men with huge tearing holes through major blood vessels, were among the earliest brought in. Some had injuries from multiple gunshot wounds, and several agents, like Risenhoover, owed their lives to flak jackets and bulletproof vests. Others had shrapnel wounds or had been hit by ricochets.

The agent with the head wound died within minutes, and two other agents were pronounced dead at Hillcrest Baptist after arrival. A few injured agents were also taken to the Providence Health Center and one was pronounced dead there, boosting the ATF death toll to four.

The dead were: twenty-eight-year-old Todd W. McKeehan, a bachelor from Elizabethton, Tennessee, who raced cars and boats, had served with the Marine Corps Reserve in Operation Desert Storm, and was attached to the ATF field office in Houston; thirty-two-year-old Steven David Willis, a Houston native who had been a special agent for three years with the U.S. Department of Defense before joining the ATF; thirty-year-old Conway LaBleu, who grew up in Lake Charles, Louisiana, was married, had a stepson, and worked out of the New Orleans ATF office; and Robb Williams, who worked out of the bureau's Little Rock office and was from Brandon, Mississippi, where he had played high school football. Williams died the day before his twenty-seventh birthday.

It was the most terrible day in the history of the federal law enforcement agency. Eventual estimates would indicate that some ten thousand rounds of ammunition were fired during the clash.

While doctors and nurses struggled to stabilize the injured and keep them alive with blood and intravenous solutions, cleaned and sutured wounds, set broken bones, and administered injections to fight pain and infection, alarming reports were broadcast by radio and television that carloads of heavily armed cultists were on their way to Waco to shoot up the hospital. A platoon of grim-faced officers from the Waco Police Department, armed with scatterguns and 9-mm pistols, was rushed to the hospital and took up positions to hold off the invasion just in case the reports were true. Other Waco police officers were posted at Providence. The reports, however, were false. Almost all the cultists were holed up inside their compound.

Meanwhile, ATF officials continued to maintain their contact and to negotiate with the barricaded cultists. An occasional shot was still fired from the compound, but there was no new serious outbreak of fighting.

Shortly before 3:00 P.M., ATF negotiators contacted executives at Dallas–Fort Worth radio station KRLD and asked them to allow the broadcast of a joint statement from the bureau and from Koresh. The station was one of the cult leader's favorites. At 4:15 the first of three broadcasts of the statement was made. An ATF spokesman assured the cultists during the broadcast that the raiding team wasn't planning to lead a new assault on the compound.

But the truce was too shaky. At almost exactly 5:00 P.M., three male cult members showed up in front of the complex and the shooting started again. The ATF spokesman hadn't promised that the agents wouldn't defend themselves. This time it was the cultists who were outgunned. A man wearing camouflage pants and firing a handgun was hit and stumbled away. Agents swarmed over another Branch Davidian and captured him after he suffered a minor wound. The man, who was armed with a .22-caliber pistol and ninety-nine rounds of ammunition, said his name was Delroy "Norman" Nash. The third man escaped.

Nash, a twenty-eight-year-old bachelor from Jamaica, was hustled off to the McLennan County Jail in Waco and held on preliminary charges of firearms violations. Charges of attempted murder of a federal agent were later added to the initial count. A few weeks after the man's arrest, authorities disclosed his real name was believed to be Norman Washington Allison.

Several hours later Texas Rangers arrested sixty-three-year-old Woodrow Kendrick after he showed up cold, wet, and exhausted at a mobile home occupied by another Branch Davidian who lived approximately four miles outside the compound. The bespectacled man, who had a history of heart problems, didn't put up any resistance. Law officers confiscated an RG .32-caliber pistol and a 9-mm Beretta while making the arrest.

Kendrick had been part of the commune since 1966, although he had been staying for about a year at an automative shop called the Mag Bag six miles away. The handyman's daughter, Kathy, had been raised in the cult but had broken away. She was the ex-wife of David Jones, who was shot in the buttocks during the gun battle.

The body of twenty-nine-year-old Michael Schroeder was spotted from a helicopter a few days after the second outbreak of gunplay, lying in a woods about 350 yards behind the house. A semiautomatic rifle was still clutched in the dead man's hand. Schroeder, whose legal wife, Kathy, and her four children were inside the compound, was the final member of the trio involved in the second shootout with the federal agents.

A half hour after the second skirmish the situation had quieted down once more, and telephone negotiations were resumed. The ATF asked KRLD to broadcast their promise to permit the barricaded cultists to give up peacefully. Instead, Koresh demanded he be allowed to broadcast portions of the Scriptures over KRLD. The ATF and station authorities agreed, and the broadcast began at 7:00 P.M.

The Scripture reading was still under way when Cable News Network, CNN, broadcast a live interview with Koresh that was punctuated by frequent groaning and apparent moans of pain from the Prophet. He claimed he was the most seriously injured of any of the Davidians, and talked of his concern for his flock.

"There are a lot of children here. I've had a lot of babies these past two years," he said. "It's true that I do have a lot of children and I do have a lot of wives." He said a two-year-old girl was killed inside one of the buildings. Asked if the girl was one of his own children, he refused to answer. Later, however, he claimed she was.

The doomsday Prophet again blamed the ATF for starting the fight and said it was only after the intruders began shooting that some of the Mighty Men had returned the fire. Although he admitted collecting an arsenal of weapons, he said he never had planned to use them.

"I was hollering, 'Go away, there are women and children here. Let's talk,' " he said of his reputed efforts to calm down the invaders. And he claimed he was aware ahead of time that the commune was about to be raided. "I knew they were coming. I knew they were coming before they knew they were coming."

Koresh also revealed during the ragged monologue that he had telephoned his mother, Bonnie Haldeman, at her home in Chandler, Texas, and told her what had happened. "I said, 'Momma, they got me. Remember, I don't hold anything against you. You know, they just don't want to hear the truth,' " he said he told her.

Koresh promised to allow two children to leave the compound every time his religious harangue was broadcast by KRLD.

The dramatic telephone interview with the injured cult leader lasted twenty-five minutes. The Scripture reading droned on until nearly two o'clock the next morning.

At that time the Dallas–Fort Worth radio station broadcast its own exclusive interview with Koresh. His voice was weak and shaky, but he sounded stubborn and determined. Again he blamed the government agents for the gun battle and said it had been unnecessary.

A baby was crying in the background as Koresh groaned and forced out the words.

"I've been shot. I'm bleeding bad," he croaked. "I'm going home. I'm going back to my father."

By that time, reinforcements were arriving and others were on the way in a fleet of cars, vans, and trucks to back up the ATF agents already ringing the compound. ATF agents from cities around the South and Southwest, dozens of Texas Rangers, an elite police weapons team, a bomb squad, an FBI hostage rescue team from Quantico, Virginia, and an armored personnel carrier from Fort Hood were hurried to the scene of the shootout. By midnight more than three hundred law officers were gathered there and more were on the way. The scene was being set for a long siege.

The news media were also flooding to the scene, and more than two hundred reporters and technicians and editors soon gathered about a mile from the compound. Authorities ordered them to move nearly a mile further away. No one could tell if another battle might break out.

By then, Koresh had released four children from the compound. Two youngsters left around 9:00 P.M., and two others about an hour later. None of them were injured.

It was the beginning of a marathon and deadly serious chess game between Koresh and a small army of federal law enforcement agents played out with the lives of children and other cult members.

# CHAPTER TWO

# The Branch Davidians

VICTOR T. HOUTEFF WAS A STUBBORN, DE-
termined man of strong religious convictions, a
firm belief that only he could find the right path
to God and heavenly reward, and a fierce intol-
erance of anyone who disagreed with him.

Born in Bulgaria in 1886, like most of his
countrymen at that time he was raised as a
member of the Eastern Orthodox Church. For a
time it was a partnership that worked. He was
faithful in his attendance, fervent in his prayer,
and as a young man he immersed himself in the

religious teachings of the priests of the church and of the Holy Writ.

He took his theological scholarship and conviction of his own authoritative insight so seriously, however, that when he differed with leading ecclesiastics on certain doctrines and spiritual philosophy, he wound up leaving the church. The church wouldn't change its doctrine for him; and he wouldn't budge for the church.

Houteff not only left the church, in fact, he also said good-bye to Bulgaria and emigrated to the United States. And after a bit of nomadic sampling of his promising new home he wound up a few miles south of Wisconsin in Rockford, Illinois.

Even in those early days when the Midwest was still much more agrarian, Rockford was a brawny, bustling city with burgeoning industry and a growing pool of workers for its factories and shops. And although it couldn't boast of the mountains of Bulgaria, and was landlocked without a body of water on its border like the Black Sea, the weather and seasons at least provided a comforting reminder of his homeland.

Houteff went into the hotel business.

His self-confidence and willingness to work hard served him well and he made a good living. But his break with Eastern Orthodoxy had left a troubling vacuum in his life. His strong sense of spirituality and religious yearnings eventually led him to a tent meeting organized by evangelists for the Seventh-Day Adventist Church. It was 1918 and it seemed his religious exile was over. The expatriot Bulgarian realized he had found a new spiritual home.

Seventh-Day Adventists shared neither the priesthood nor the ritual of Eastern Orthodoxy. But Houteff liked the strict, clean-living devotion of the members and the literal interpretation of the Bible of his new church, which was so dramatically illustrated by its insistence on celebrating the seventh day of the week as the Sabbath. The choice of a Saturday Sabbath provided the denomination with half of its name.

A firm belief in the Second Coming of Christ, the Second Advent, provided the other half. Houteff believed strongly in that, and in the coming destruction of evil in the world and triumph of good as prophesied to the apostle John in Revelation, the last book of the Bible.

As religious converts tend to do, Houteff plunged into a zealous study of his new faith. And he continued his theological scholarship after moving across the country to Los Angeles, where he was appointed assistant superintendent of a Seventh-Day Adventist Church Sabbath school. Approximately two hundred students attended the school.

When Houteff wasn't actively teaching, he helped support himself by selling Maytag washing machines. But as he taught and peddled washing machines, he continued to pore over the teachings of William Miller, a onetime Baptist layman who preached in New York State and who, though he had died thirty-seven years before Houteff's birth, was in many ways much like Houteff himself. Miller was also a fervid student of the Bible, especially the prophecies in the Old Testament Book of Daniel and the New Testament Book of Revelation.

Eventually Miller's readings and theological grapplings had led him to the conclusion that the world would end sometime between March 21, 1843, and March 21, 1844.

Miller based his computations on Daniel 8:14, which states: "For two thousand and three hundred evenings and mornings; then the sanctuary shall be restored to its rightful state."

Miller—as many students of the Bible still do—interpreted scriptural references to a "day" to be symbolic of a year. He began his figuring from 457 B.C., the date Daniel is believed to have written his prophecy and the date Jerusalem was destroyed. Treating the 457 as a negative, he determined that doomsday would occur 2,300 years after the holy city was leveled—in 1843.

Those were turbulent, worrisome times of

strong fundamentalist religious belief for Americans. Less than a decade earlier, a motley collection of patriots, frontiersmen, and gunfighters had been massacred by a superior force of Mexicans at the Battle of the Alamo, and Texas had proclaimed its independence.

By the mid-1840s, adventurous settlers were just beginning to make their way across the Oregon Trail to farm, log the broad stands of virgin timber, and to raise families in the Great Northwest. And in 1844 inventor Samuel F. B. Morse sent the first message by telegraph from Washington to Baltimore. The message asked: "What hath God wrought?"

Even before Morse tapped out his historic message, Miller believed he had a good idea what God was up to. The New York State preacher and those who later accepted his teachings were convinced that during the cataclysmic times leading to the Apocalypse, truly devout Christians would be sorted out from the rest of mankind and permitted to participate in the Second Coming.

Thousands of people who believed that Miller's calculations were correct sold their property and household possessions, gave them to neighbors, or left crops to rot in the fields and simply rode away on their horses and in their buggies to wait for Christ's return and the end of the world. Their neighbors and the press called them "Millerites," and they also accepted that name as well as "Adventists" for a while.

During a single week, one thousand Millerites were baptized by the pastors of a single church. Many of the faithful dressed in white robes and waited on New England hilltops for the Lord to reach down and lift them into heaven. Pinnacle Hill in Rochester, New York, drew thousands of zealous believers waiting to be lifted to heaven. Stories spread in the skeptical press about fanatical Millerites dressed in ascencion robes who climbed to the tops of houses and trees or congregated in cemeteries for weird rites.

The Millerites were disappointed when the world didn't end in 1843, the date initially calculated for the coming of glory. Over nearly two years, the desperate prophet set four different dates for doomsday. But when 1844 passed and the sun continued to come up in the morning and to go down at night as usual, his followers broke away and gave up on the discredited sage of Low Hampton.

Newspaper columnists and reporters made a circus out of their disappointment, and the doomsdayers were ridiculed by former neighbors and family who had refused to share their belief in the Second Coming. Many of the crestfallen faithful, however, weren't ready to abandon the Adventist movement and all of Miller's teachings. They decided he might have been wrong about the time frame of his End Time prediction, but he wasn't wrong about the ultimate truth of an eventual Second Coming.

Those who still believed formed splinter Adventist groups that shared more of the basic doctrinal beliefs than feathery differences over fine-line biblical interpretations. The largest group eventually to emerge was the Seventh-Day Adventist Church, which formed in 1863, the year President Abraham Lincoln issued the Emancipation Proclamation and read the Gettysburg Address. Like most of the other Adventists, they avoided repeating Miller's mistake and didn't predict a specific doomsday date.

Firm in the conviction that the body is a temple where the Holy Spirit resides, the Seventh-Day Adventists have set severe restrictions on how the corporeal sheath can be treated. Devout followers of church doctrine do not eat, drink, or otherwise ingest anything that might be harmful to the body. The teachings of the denomination do not permit smoking, the drinking of alcoholic beverages, tea, or coffee, or the eating of some meats.

Despite their acceptance of biblical warnings of a final battle between good and evil, Seventh-Day Adventists do not believe in fighting or waging war themselves. Their young men are conscientious objectors, and when Adventists do serve in the military they fill noncombat roles such as doctors, nurses, and field medics. Church doctrine, nevertheless, permits members to own firearms, to hunt, and to target practice.

Seventh-Day Adventists also support a spirited missionary program to spread the gospel and attract new converts. They believe that Christ cannot return until people around the world have heard the true Word.

By the early 1990s, 160 years after its founding, the Seventh-Day Adventist Church has a worldwide membership of more than five million. About 780,000 members live in the United States and Canada, where there are four thousand churches, including three in Waco. But there are also strong Adventist communities in England, Australia, and in some Caribbean island nations.

The modern church is a conservative mainline Protestant denomination with national headquarters in Silver Spring, Maryland, and its own publishing house. For the most part the membership is composed of peaceful, clean-living men and women who stress health and education and take an active, positive role in their communities. They make good neighbors. In that respect they are still the same as they were fifty years ago, when Houteff was teaching at one of their schools.

As a teacher, he was generous about passing on to his students and to other members of the church his interpretation of the Book of Daniel and of the vivid symbolism and chilling prophecy of Revelation—even though some of his views broadly differed from accepted Seventh-Day Adventist teachings. His personalized concepts about events preceding the Apocalypse, the return of Jesus, and the beginning of the millennium were especially at odds with church doctrine. Another break between Houteff and his church was inevitable.

When Seventh-Day Adventist leaders accused him of disrupting the school, they were met with even more stubborn resistance than he had demonstrated when he was challenged over his views of Eastern Orthodoxy.

In 1930 Houteff issued a jarring statement that outlined his interpretation of the prophecies and demanded major reforms in church doctrine. He asserted that he had been selected by God to cleanse the church of hypocrites and false believers. Houteff called his alarming manifesto The Shepherd's Rod. The reaction of church leaders to Houteff's outrageous declaration was only slightly more benign than the reaction of the pope during the early sixteenth century when

Martin Luther posted his Ninety-five Theses in Wittenberg and set off the Protestant Reformation.

No one called for Houteff to be burned at the stake. Nevertheless, he had clearly developed insoluble differences with church credo. In 1934 he was disenfranchised from the Seventh-Day Adventists and left, taking more than a dozen families with him. His converts believed he was a prophet inspired by the Holy Word. Borrowing the name of the statement submitted to the elders of his former church, he called his breakaway sect The Shepherd's Rod.

The title of the manifesto and name of the new sect was apparently taken from Micah 6:9 of the King James Version of the Bible, which says: "The Lord's voice crieth unto the city, and the man of wisdom shall see thy name: hear ye the Rod, and Who hath appointed it."

Among the more important tenets of Houteff's teachings was his belief that in the final days, God would purge everyone from the church except the most faithful. He drew much of this conviction from Ezekiel 9 and from Revelation 7. A terrifying vision of God dispatching six death angels to kill everyone in Jerusalum who hasn't been marked on the forehead with a cross is described in Ezekiel. And Revelation tells of another vision in which the foreheads of 144,000 people are marked. Houteff was convinced that those elite 144,000 true believers, were those who would be spared by the dark angels spoken of in Ezekiel.

The members of The Shepherd's Rod continued to worship for a few months in Los Angeles, then in 1935 the tiny flock followed their prophet across the country to the windswept prairie land of central Texas. They purchased nearly two hundred acres of ranchland a couple of miles outside Waco in the heart of Baptist country. They named the desolate spread on the chalky hills near old Lake Waco the Mount Carmel Center and settled down to wait for the End Times and the Second Coming of Christ. Houteff explained that careful study of the Scriptures had enabled him to select Waco as their new home.

Like most of their neighbors, they lived simply, working the land, planting crops, and raising a herd of fine dairy cattle while studying the Gospels and spending long hours in intense prayer. Eventually they even established their own printing plant. Houteff and his industrious flock kept to themselves and the sect grew slowly. By 1940, although the religious commune doubled its property holdings with the purchase of another 188 acres of land, there still were only sixty-four people living in the reclusive religious commune.

Houteff became convinced that King David's regal dominion was about to be restored in Palestine, and in 1942 he devised a new name for the sect. They became the Davidian Seventh-Day Adventists. At about the same time, the prophet advised his followers that they should prepare themselves for the Second Coming of Christ to occur in less than a year.

Allied troops invaded Europe, the Japanese fleet was destroyed, and nearly three years after the date set in Houteff's doomsday prediction, Italy, Germany, and Japan had toppled like dominoes. By 1945 World War II had ended, without the help of the pacifist members of the religious commune. Now the Cold War was beginning— and life was continuing at Mount Carmel. And the Messiah hadn't returned.

But the sect had other troubles. Although their community was slowly growing, many new members had joined at the expense of their marriages, giving up spouses who disagreed with the sect's grim apocalyptic credo. Houteff was dead set against members of his flock hanging on to spouses or marrying outsiders who weren't practicing Davidians.

And the Davidians' school was closed after a lecherous schoolmaster got into trouble for having sex with several of his girl students. After that, despite the reluctance of the solitary community to have many dealings with outsiders, the children of cult members attended public school classes with children from the Waco area.

At last, in 1955, their faith was shaken once more when Houteff died. It was an event that most, possibly all, the members of the devout religious commune hadn't believed would occur. They had expected that he would live on to reign over the new kingdom of God.

Houteff's wife, Florence, succeeded him as the new spiritual pathfinder. But she made the same mistake so many other Adventist prophets before her had made. She announced a specific date for doomsday. Sister Florence announced that the new kingdom would be created on April 22, 1959. In a divine bloodletting, Seventh-Day Adventists who were not following the path of righteousness would be slaughtered along with others who had strayed from the path, and only the chosen faithful would survive into the millennium, she declared.

The date coincided with Passover, the Jewish religious holiday commemorating the Exodus, when Moses lead the children of Israel across the Red Sea and out of bondage in Egypt.

The jarring announcement was picked up by the press and widely circulated around the country. Once again, people began getting rid of their personal property, selling or giving away businesses, quitting jobs, spending long hours in Bible study and prayer as they prepared themselves for the End Times. Hundreds of new believers journeyed to Mount Carmel and joined the prophetess's religious community. Membership eventually swelled to around fourteen hundred people.

Some of the late prophet's most die-hard loyalists began to discuss the possibility of Victor Houteff's resurrection. Perhaps their late leader hadn't been slated to reign over the new kingdom after all; perhaps he would fulfill the role of Elijah, and his miraculous return from the grave would signal the Advent.

Waco was also undergoing growing pains at the time the new converts were making their way to Mount Carmel to wait for the Second Coming. While the city limits expanded, the one-time cow town was moving too close to the religious settlement for the comfort of the Davidians. Then the state government began condemning land to make room for the new Lake Waco. Florence Houteff sold the property for a generous seven hundred thousand dollars and bought a new nine-hundred-acre spread on a stretch of isolated prairie land about twelve miles east of the city.

The new Mount Carmel was closer to Elk and to Axtell than it was to Waco. Each of these flyspeck-size settlements was about four miles from the Davidians' new home and were so small they didn't even show up on many road maps. The Davidians' new home offered exactly the kind of privacy and isolation they were looking for while waiting for Jesus to take them to heaven. As they waited, they grew crops, tended farm animals, and threw up a few flimsy buildings that would shield them from the the cold, rain, and snow during the brief time they expected to stay there. And they continued their Bible studies, fasted, and prayed.

After the 1959 Passover holiday passed uneventfully, most of the newcomers, and some of the more longtime members, packed up their meager belongings and began drifting away from Mount Carmel. Florence Houteff's doomsday prophecy was a devastating miscalculation, and by early May less than a third of the Adventists who had once gathered at Mount Carmel were still there. Most of the survivors were either planning to strike out on their own or were busy forming new splinter groups.

Eventually even the disgraced prophetess herself left Mount Carmel. The few faithful holdouts who remained were forced to sell off all but about one hundred acres of the commune's former holdings.

A charismatic, bearded man with a deep voice and commanding manner named Benjamin Roden attracted the largest group of followers to his leadership. An authoritative scholar of the Bible, Roden was from the West Texas city of Odessa. Still a devoted Adventist, he named the new sect the Branch. "Get off the dead rod," he advised, "and move onto a living branch." Roden declared himself the successor to the biblical King David.

Roden was wise enough to resist any possible temptation to make a definitive prediction of when doomsday would occur. He knew better than to take a chance on an embarrassing re-enactment of his predecessor's devastating bumble that the loyal few who remained referred to as the "Great Disappointment."

The most significant event of his leadership was the establishment of a commune in Israel. He moved there for a while with his family and several followers, but eventually returned to Texas. When he died at Mount Carmel in 1978, his wife, Lois, was elevated to the role of prophetess.

At first the changeover didn't set off a power struggle, and it was assumed at that time by most of the Branch Davidians at Mount Carmel that when Lois finally moved on to glory she would be succeeded by her son, George.

But they hadn't counted on Vernon Howell, an aggressive, bright, curly-haired young convert who had a lust for power and women.

# CHAPTER THREE

# A Power Struggle

WHEN VERNON HOWELL JOINED THE
Branch Davidians in 1983, he was trouble waiting to happen.

The good-looking, long-haired twenty-three-
year-old rock musician was a born rebel and a
born leader. He was intelligent, aggressive, am-
bitious, and determined. He had the easy, confident spiel of a courtroom lawyer, or of a
television evangelist. And he knew the Bible. He
had a photographic memory and could recite

chapter and verse of the Old Testament without omitting a word of the text.

Howell was a twelve-year-old schoolboy living in the Dallas suburb of Richardson when he sat down and memorized the New Testament. But he did much more than merely memorize the Scriptures. He could pick out a phrase, a sentence, or a word in Proverbs, Ezekiel, Daniel, Revelation, or any other chapter of the Good Book and discuss the esoterics and meaning for twenty minutes—or for hours.

And the articulate young man could handle himself equally well during the spirited discussions that were such an important part of life in the religious community, discussions that dealt with the apocalyptic writings and preachments of Miller or Houteff and of other early Davidian prophets.

No one could really hold his own in debates or discussions with Howell—especially not George B. Roden. Roden was simply no match for the encyclopedic knowledge or the runaway mouth of the would-be rock music star who had joined the religious community with such a disruptive splash.

The bad blood between the newcomer and Roden, the heir apparent to the role of the living prophet, began to show up almost immediately after Howell arrived. The religious commune that people around the area spoke of variously as Mount Carmel and as Rodenville was already experiencing troubled times. Sister Roden had shaken up her flock by announcing that the Holy Spirit was female. When she led prayer she called on "Our Mother, who art in heaven."

Sister Roden and her son had also tangled so bitterly over control of the property and of the sect, which after her ascension was once again renamed and called the Living Waters Branch, that she had been forced to take their quarrel to outsiders. She had to file a lawsuit in the McLennan County courts to hold off his claim that he was the Messiah and consequently entitled to the leadership role.

Even after the courts ruled in his mother's favor, George didn't give up and continued his struggle for supremacy in the courts and at Mount Carmel. Meanwhile, mother and son each remained in the compound, each claiming to be the one with divine inspiration.

But George didn't have the powerful appeal of his father. His behavior was too erratic and eccentric for most of the Davidians at Mount Carmel to accept, and Sister Roden remained in shaky control. There seemed to be no limit to George's ambition, however. In 1976 as the feud with his mother was just heating up, he threw his hat in the ring for nomination as the Democratic candidate for president of the United States. He was beaten by Jimmy Carter and several other candidates.

The timing of Howell's appearance couldn't have been better for the would-be prophet. The Davidians weren't exactly rudderless, but Sister Roden's authority was eroding and quite a few members of the commune were convinced her son wasn't the leader to step into the breach and take over after her death.

From the very first after his arrival, Howell admitted he was a sinner. He seemed, in fact, to revel in the knowledge of his iniquities and unabashedly shared even the most personal details of his sins with other Davidians. He confessed, among other acknowledged trespasses against the Word, that he simply couldn't stop masturbating.

Howell's glib admission touched the heart of Sister Roden. The severe, angular old woman invited the slender young charmer into her bedroom. It was a move that would be debated by Branch Davidians for years to come.

George Roden was outraged! He accused Howell of raping Lois. He was convinced that the mouthy interloper's new sleeping arrangements were part of a carefully calculated grab for power and that Howell was deliberately insinuating himself into the affections and confidence of the prophetess by using sex.

According to reports years later from former cult members, Howell explained that he was merely bowing to a commandment from God to comply with Isaiah 8:3. A portion of the Bible verse states, *"And I went unto the prophetess; and she conceived, and bare a son."*

Both Howell and the prophetess reportedly claimed at various times that she had become pregnant, as God had commanded, but had miscarried. They disagreed over the reason she lost the baby, the ex-followers said. Sister Roden blamed it on her young consort for refusing to share leadership with her. Howell claimed she miscarried because God was angry with her for passing out tithe money to her grown children.

Years later, Howell reportedly had a different story altogether to tell. He rudely denied he ever made love to Lois. She was as ugly as Medusa, he claimed.

Regardless of which version of the curious union is correct, George was right about the overall effect of it all. As the apparent consort of Sister Roden, Howell's stature within the commune and among other disciples who lived outside Mount Carmel was considerably enhanced. His mere proximity and accessibility to her gave him an authority unavailable to others, including her son.

According to later reports from Davidians who were witness to the turbulent events, Howell badgered the old woman to kick her son out of the commune. George hung on as best he could, fuming and stewing.

In the meantime, both men began gathering coteries of personal supporters around them. Howell and George agreed on hardly anything, including the interloper's relationship with Sister Roden. Another crisis within the cloistered community at Mount Carmel was rapidly shaping up.

An uneasy truce continued, however, and in 1984 Howell married fourteen-year-old Rachel Jones. The pretty bride, who had grown up at Mount Carmel, was the daughter of Perry Jones, a highly respected and long time cult elder who eventually became vice-president. Howell was twenty-four and was already thought by a considerable number of Branch Davidians to be a prophet.

Howell's link through marriage to the high-ranking father of the bride increased his stature at the commune even further. And it provided an opportunity for him to move out of Sister Roden's bedroom for good.

By that time he was confiding to anyone willing to listen that only he understood the full and true meaning of the Word of God. He claimed in fact that it had been revealed to him by divine revelation that he would become the seventh angel of God and set off the events leading to the Apocalypse. Sister Roden no longer had her inspiration, he said.

The old woman knew about the backstabbing but couldn't do anything about it. She glumly admitted that her former consort was taking charge of the religious sect.

George, a husky, heavily bearded man with piercing eyes, began stomping around Mount Carmel with an Uzi slung over his shoulder or swinging from his belt. The peace-loving Davidians had never tolerated firearms there before, not even so much as a beebee gun. The drastic change in the atmosphere at the compound was troubling, and fear increased within the already tense community.

Sister Roden died in 1986, and the stage was set at last for settlement of the long-festering rivaly between Howell and her son, George. Backed by about a dozen loyalists, most of them elderly, Roden forced his adversary out of the compound at gunpoint. In control of Mount Carmel at last, George announced that, like his father before him, he was the Living Prophet.

Banished from Mount Carmel, Howell led his

wife and a handful of followers drifting here and there through Texas, like the children of Israel wandering through the wilderness.

Occasionally he traveled to California to meet with supporters there. Donald and Jeannine Bunds, a couple who lived with their son and daughter in Highland Park, a comfortable upper-income neighborhood of Los Angeles, were two of the most faithful.

Donald Bunds was an engineer, his wife a nurse. Although they had never moved into Mount Carmel, they visited the commune and had faithfully tithed through the years the Branch Davidians were led by Benjamin and Lois Roden.

Tithing wasn't enough for Howell, however. He demanded not only more money, but other commitments as well. When Howell's group needed a better means of transportation, the Bunds bought them a ten-thousand-dollar van.

Sometime after that, Howell told them he wanted a house in the area where the Davidian men could stay during their trips to California. The Bunds bought a nice house in Pomona with a handsome rock facing that Howell particularly liked. It was worth a hundred thousand dollars.

The Bunds' son seemed to get along well enough with Howell, but their pretty dark-haired daughter, Robyn, didn't like him. A classic California girl, she resented his frequent visits to their home and the increasing control he was developing over her family. Finally, when she was seventeen, Robyn moved across the country to stay with relatives in New Bedford, Massachusetts.

Howell sometimes mixed business with pleasure while he was in California keeping his membership in line, proselytizing recruits, and preaching. Hard rock music was still a big part of his life and he sometimes cruised local clubs trying to pick up good-looking women by dazzling them with a combination of his dimpled good looks, his charm, and talk about how females should be given more of an active role in religion.

Although California was a rich area to mine for converts and cash, Howell realized that his destiny was in Texas and had settled his weary flock in the appropriately named town of Palestine in rural Anderson County.

In Palestine, a community of about fourteen thousand people, the near-penniless nomads squatted in plywood packing boxes, a few tents, and flimsy lean-tos set up in the piney woods at the edge of town.

A few months after Robyn Bunds moved to New Bedford she got homesick and telephoned her parents. She wanted to return to California.

They told her she couldn't come home. Vernon needed her in Texas. So the pretty teenager traveled to Palestine and moved into a small tent with another cult member, Michelle Tom, a young woman from Australia.

It seemed to Robyn, after she joined the Davidian splinter group among the piney woods and jackrabbits of East Texas, that somehow a miraculous metamorphosis had changed Howell. He was nothing like the bumbling jerk she previously had considered him to be. She was impressed with how much warmer, more considerate, and capable he had become. He never stumbled over words, and he was refined, organized, and smooth.

But it was miserable living in the primitive settlement, especially in the winter with no heat, hot water, or indoor plumbing. Robyn telephoned her parents and begged to come home. They took her back to California, but after a while she returned to Palestine. And a short time after her return to the fold, the Prophet made love to her. She was seventeen. He explained that the physical communion they had shared made her his wife, even though he was still married to Rachel.

Jeannine Bunds didn't learn about the unorthodox wedding until about six months later, when she traveled to Palestine to observe Passover with her daughter and other residents of the commune. When Robyn told her parents she was sleeping with the Living Prophet and was his wife, they were upset. When they confronted Howell about the situation, however, he met their complaints by explaining that her daughter had been chosen to bear children for God.

By the time Howell first took Robyn into his bed, he and Rachel had become the parents of a boy, Cyrus, born in 1987. Howell's firstborn son's name was borrowed from the Persian emperor who defeated Babylon and freed the Jews from captivity in 539 B.C. Two years after their son was born, Rachel gave birth to a girl. They named her Star.

Despite his son's impressive name, Howell was mean to Cyrus, as well as to other children in the growing flock, former supporters later claimed. He didn't like to be crossed and wouldn't put up with resistance from anyone, even children who didn't realize the serious trouble that even the slightest infraction could get them into. At various times he beat Cyrus and withheld food, and before the pink-cheeked and curly-haired little boy was even old enough to begin attending school, Howell would make him sleep by himself on a bench in a garage after scaring him with terrifying stories about huge rats.

The tug-of-war with Roden over the membership and property of the Davidians at Mount Carmel, hadn't ended when Howell and his small band of followers were banished from the compound. Howell was plotting a return. And Roden's leadership would continue to be shaky as long as the breakaway Davidians were camped a hundred miles east of Mount Carmel.

Roden complained a few times to state and federal authorities that his rival was up to no good and was a dangerous man. Nothing happened.

So he took the initiative and made a desperate move. He challenged his rival to a bizarre contest designed to prove which of them was the more worthy and divinely inspired. Roden proposed that whichever of the two claimants to the leadership was able to resurrect a former cult member from the dead should be recognized as the Living Prophet.

Howell was too sly to risk another embarrassing debacle like the Great Disappointment, and he rejected the absurd challenge.

Roden began putting the macabre plan in motion anyway. He had the coffin of Anna Hughes, an eighty-five-year-old cult member who had died twenty years earlier, dug up from the Mount Carmel Cemetery and began working on her resurrection. A flag imprinted with the Star of David on a blue field was draped over the coffin and the altar it rested on. Then the would-be Messiah implored and shouted out invocations and petitions over it for days, calling for divine intercession to restore the old woman's life. He ended at least one prayer by invoking his own name, "George B. Roden." Even then, however, nothing happened.

Howell responded to the would-be resurrectionist's frustrating efforts by going to the police. He notified McLennan County sheriff's officers in Waco that Roden was abusing a corpse.

On Halloween Day, sheriff's deputies told county prosecutors what was going on at Mount Carmel. Prosecutors responded by explaining that no charges could be filed without some evidence that there was actually a corpse in the coffin.

When Howell was notified of the problem, he reputedly decided to take a photograph of the old woman's bones inside the coffin. In the early-morning hours of November 3, 1987, Howell, Paul Fatta, and six other male companions slipped past the hulks of junked cars and trash that littered the approach to Mount Carmel and into the darkened compound. They were dressed in camouflage clothes and were heavily armed.

The interlopers crouched quietly in the shadows as the residents of Mount Carmel awoke and busied themselves with their usual mundane chores, prayer, and other activities that marked the beginning of their new day. At last, after school-age children and the adults who worked outside had left the compound, the band of armed men began drifting into the ramshackle buildings. The surprised occupants were advised to clear out; there was a good possibility that serious trouble was about to erupt.

A Roden loyalist hurried into George's quarters and told him what was going on. The leader responded by snatching up an Uzi and rushing out the door. Seconds later he and the invaders were blazing away at each other. It was almost like the Wild West gunfights in old Waco, except that the nineteenth-century cow-town roughnecks and yahoos had used six-shooters instead of Uzis and semiautomatic rifles.

By the time McLennan County sheriff's deputies were alerted by neighbors and intervened in the fierce shootout about twenty-minutes after it began, Roden had suffered wounds from a bullet that grazed the fingers of his right hand and smashed into his chest. Eighteen bullet holes riddled a tree he had hidden behind. Somehow, in what must have seemed miraculous to some of the devout women and older members who had stayed behind at the compound that day, no one was killed.

The sheriff's officers stepped into the violent internecine fracas by making a telephone call to the compound. They talked to Howell and asked him to stop shooting and surrender. He agreed to the request, and Sheriff Harwell and a deputy drove out to the compound. Howell and his raiders peacefully turned over their weapons, including five semiautomatic assault rifles, two shotguns, and nearly three thousand rounds of ammunition.

Howell and his fellow gunfighters from Palestine were hauled back to Waco and charged with attempted murder. But they were quickly freed on bond and permitted to return to their encampment in Anderson County. Roden was patched up by doctors, but he was left with bullet fragments in his chest that were expected to remain there the rest of his life.

Despite his injuries, the forty-nine-year-old Roden might have emerged as the winner of the violent face-off over the cult's leadership if he hadn't made another terrible blunder that had nothing to do with the shootout.

He was still filing motions and appeals in federal and state courts linked to the old feud over stewardship of the membership and property of the Branch Davidians. And when the Texas State Supreme Court crossed him, he responded by filing legal motions intimating that

God might step into the squabble on his side and inflict the justices with AIDS and herpes. A former prosecutor, speaking years later to a reporter for *Newsweek*, recalled that the motions were some of the most obscene and profane documents ever filed in a federal courthouse.

Roden was charged with contempt of court and sentenced to six months behind bars.

Howell didn't waste any time taking advantage of his opportunity. The long travail in the wilderness was over. He and his followers packed up their gear and moved into Mount Carmel.

Even with Roden temporarily out of the way, Howell and his seven companions in the raid on Mount Carmel had their own problem in court to deal with. When their trial finally began in the McLennan County Courthouse early in 1988, Howell admitted firing a gun in Roden's direction but said he was aiming at a tree. His supporters weren't aiming their guns at anyone either, he claimed, but had fired them into the air. It was all a show of power aimed at spooking Roden into giving up, he said.

Roden was brought from his cell at the McLennan County Jail to testify in the third-floor courtroom. His offer to resurrect Anna Hughes brought an especially ghoulish aspect to the already bizarre trial when her casket was brought into the third-floor hallway. When the casket was removed at the end of the day, the old woman's bones hadn't stirred. She was still at rest and unresurrected.

Howell and his comrades made a better impression on the jury. They showed up for the court proceedings dressed in neat business suits, with neckties and polished shoes. The leader's thick, long, curly hair was neatly styled, and he looked more like a conservative young businessman than a crazed cultist who had allegedly led a commando-style raid on a peaceful religious compound filled with women, children, and a handful of old men.

The defendants were trailed to the courthouse by a crowd of fervent supporters from Mount Carmel, including Rachel and Robyn. Most of the women were dressed as modestly as old-time celibate Shakers, without makeup, and some had their hair braided or pulled back in severe buns. Several of the women carried babies in their arms or held on to the hands of toddlers. Robyn recalled years later to reporters how touched she was as she watched Vernon standing beside Rachel, their little girl, Star, in his arms while tears streamed down his cheeks.

Howell's seven companions in the raid on Mount Carmel were acquitted, but the jury was unable to reach a verdict in the leader's case. After voting nine to three for his acquittal, a mistrial was declared, and the charges were ultimately dropped by the McLennan County district attorney's office.

After the announcement of the hung jury, a couple of the jurors walked across the courtroom and hugged the former defendant. Some of the jurors said they believed the troubles at Mount Carmel basically involved a feud over property. And of the two primary rivals, they believed Roden was the more dangerous.

Standing beside his lawyer, Gary Coker, Jr., and beaming with pleasure, Howell invited everyone—judge, defense attorneys, prosecutors, other court officers, and the jury—out to Mount Carmel for an ice-cream social.

Once he was back at Mount Carmel he explained to any of his followers who hadn't already figured it out for themselves that the innocent verdicts and the mistrial were just more examples of his divine inspiration and favor.

To nearby ranchers, farmers, and other neighbors who had bemusedly watched the rowdy high jinks going on among the Davidians, it appeared that the cultists were at last settling down once more.

But the Davidians were about to experience still more radical upheavals—in their Christian beliefs and in their personal lives.

# CHAPTER FOUR

# The Living Prophet

*Beware of false prophets, which come to you in sheep's clothing, but inwardly they are ravening wolves.*

*—Matthew 7:15*

CHANGES AT MOUNT CARMEL AFTER HOWell took over were rapid, dramatic, and forever altered the lives and creed of the faithful flock who followed the new Living Prophet.

Howell moved off to a fast start, making major physical changes at the compound and in the direction the spiritual lives of his disciples were to take.

The abandoned car hulks and trash that littered the compound were hauled away. Some of the flimsier buildings were burned or torn down and rebuilt or replaced. Others were reinforced with concrete. Work was begun on the passageways and tunnels connecting buildings, and a guard tower was erected near the center of the compound.

Wells for water were dug, and a satellite TV dish was set up. An old school bus was even buried to become a primitive bunker and was linked to the tunnels under the budding fortress emerging from the formerly benign scatter of shacks and cottages.

There was no more talk of "Rodenville" at Mount Carmel. The sect once more became the Branch Davidians, and there was no question about who the new leader was. There were no more serious problems from the recently deposed prophet.

After Roden was freed, the bitter loser, defeated in the war for Mount Carmel by the time lost in jail and by his rival's superior strategy, wound up back in Odessa in West Texas, where his father had come from. His inner demons caught up with him once more, and in 1989 he shot and killed a fifty-six-year-old man named Wayman Dale Adair. Roden claimed Adair was an assassin dispatched by Howell to kill him. He had acted in self-defense, the deposed Living Prophet insisted.

A year later a jury returned a verdict of not

guilty by reason of insanity, and Roden was committed to a mental hospital at Vernon, Texas, about forty miles northwest of Wichita Falls. The fortresslike psychiatric hospital was a few minutes' drive from the Oklahoma state line, hundreds of miles from Mount Carmel. If Roden puzzled over the curious twist of fate that had led him to confinement in a hospital that shared a name with that of his old nemesis, he apparently never talked of it with anyone.

At Vernon, the embittered patient continued to accuse Howell of committing rape, arson, and embezzlement of the religious community's funds. He remained convinced that the new leader at Mount Carmel was a dangerous man, and filed a series of hand-scribbled lawsuits that kept Howell and his elders busy in the Texas courts. Most of the legal actions disputed ownership of various property at Mount Carmel.

Nevertheless, with his commitment to the hospital for the criminally insane, any chance that Roden might have been able to use the courts or somehow gather supporters around him and oust Howell from leadership of the Branch Davidians had gone up in smoke.

Howell was in firm control at Mount Carmel and there were no rivals to his authority. The Living Prophet had come a long way for a high school dropout who began life as the illegitimate son of an unmarried fifteen-year-old Houston girl who worked in a nursing home.

Vernon Wayne Howell was born on August 17, 1959, the same year Florence Houteff announced that Passover would usher in the new kingdom of God and led the Branch Davidians to the Great Disappointment. Twenty-year-old Bobby Howell, a carpenter, was the baby's father.

According to Bobby Howell's mother, Jean Holub, the couple stayed together for a couple of years, until her son developed an interest in another woman. After the couple broke up, the toddler was turned over to his maternal grandmother, Erline Clark, to raise. Vernon called his maternal grandmother Mama.

A few years later his mother, Bonnie, took him to live with her in San Antonio. He was six years old when he moved with his mother and stepfather, Ray Haldeman, to the Dallas area in northern Texas. They enrolled him in the Alex Sanger Elementary School in East Dallas. The little boy was dyslexic and had trouble with lessons, leading school authorities to enroll him in special classes. He never did do well in school. But he was inquisitive and handy, good at fixing broken toys and just about anything else that needed repair around the house or on the farms he sometimes lived on.

His stepfather was also a carpenter, and the

family didn't stay put. By the time Vernon was in the eighth grade he was living in Garland, Texas, where he attended the Sellers Middle School. A year later he moved up to Garland High School for his freshman year. He didn't have much to do with extracurricular activities, and later reports that he played on the football team are apparently false. But he did play for one semester with the school band.

The next year he was back in Dallas, however. He enrolled there in the Dallas Junior Academy, but he got poor grades and after less than a month had left the Seventh-Day Adventist–affiliated school. He returned to Garland for some additional schooling but never completed high school.

Despite his difficulties with school, like many dyslexic chilren, Vernon was a bright, pleasant boy. He got along well with his stepbrother, Roger, and loved animals. His boyhood was very much like that of his peers; he roamed the pastures and woods with a favorite mutt named Jet Fuel; fished in local creeks and ponds; rode farm tractors; played cowboys and Indians with toy guns; and during his tumbleweed travels around the state he made new friends easily.

School friends and family members generally considered him to be a good boy who didn't get into trouble or hang out with other youngsters who did. He was tenderhearted, and once when he and his paternal grandmother were on their way to a restaurant for a meal, he gave a ten-dollar bill to a vagrant. He solemnly explained to his grandmother that he knew what it was like to be hungry, and they had to do what they could to help others.

A young aunt recalled years later that the only bad thing she ever saw him do was blow a frog to bits with a firecracker.

Vernon got along well with other children, and as he approached his teens his dimpled good looks and natural charm made him especially popular with girls. His ability with the guitar, which he picked at and strummed during spare time, further enhanced his appeal. Sometimes he practiced late into the night with the volume turned up full blast, then finally put his guitar away and picked up his Bible.

Girls and music took a secondary place in his interests to religion and his spiritual growth. God and the Bible had dominated his interests since he was a little boy. His mother often watched him return home from school and drop to his knees beside his bed, where he lapsed into fervent prayer. Sometimes he went to the barn to pray in private, and he would remain there for hours in earnest communion with the Lord while tears rolled down his cheeks.

When he wasn't praying, he was often poring over the Bible. His mind soaked up the Scriptures like a sponge while he pondered the mystifying complexities of prophecies and parables, arcane symbolism, and intricate hidden meanings of seemingly obscure words or phrases. Just like Victor Houteff and other self-taught Bible scholars before him, he wasn't shy about sharing the conclusions he reached through his intense Bible study.

After Vernon left high school he looked up his birth father. He went to Houston, picked up a telephone book, and began dialing Howells until he found someone who could help him contact Bobby. Today Bobby Howell has six other children, but with one glaring exception the reunion with his son Vernon was pleasant. During a later interview on a Houston television station, Bobby Howell recalled the meeting and said his son had preached to him constantly while they were together. "I told him I didn't want to talk religion," the elder Howell told the KHOU-TV audience.

Also like Houteff, young Vernon's obsession with unlocking the mysteries of the Bible often led to serious conflicts over important matters of faith with elders of the Seventh-Day Adventist churches he attended.

Howell wound up in the East Texas town of

Tyler after leaving the Dallas Junior Academy, but in 1977 he moved a few miles due west to the much smaller community of Chandler. Fewer than one thousand people lived in the town. His mother worked in a nursing home there.

Two years later he joined the Seventh-Day Adventist church in Tyler and hung on to his membership for two years before he was kicked out. The long-haired young man's troubles began almost as soon as he joined the congregation. He reportedly rebelled at various personal restrictions of appearance and diet that are part of the faith, and he argued with his spiritual elders over serious matters of doctrine.

He also got into serious trouble when he approached the church's pastor, L. Hartley Berlin, with a shocking announcement. God had given the preacher's pretty teenage daughter, Sandy, to him, Howell declared. The Reverend Berlin didn't believe that for a moment and sent the brash young man packing. Distressed church leaders finally had their fill of Howell and took drastic action. They disfellowshiped him—dropping him from their roles.

Lynn Ray, a church elder, told the *Tyler Morning Telegraph* years later that the boy was bright but was rowdy and wouldn't accept instruction from anyone. "He was a bad influence on young people in our church," Ray declared.

Cyril Miller, president of the Adventists' Southwestern Union Theology Center, was even more bluntly critical when he talked to a news reporter about the former church member. "He was a kook, a genuine religious fanatic that was almost totally irrational," Miller declared.

Howell was eighteen years old when he cleared out of Tyler and headed for greener pastures, intent on continuing his spiritual odyssey while seeking fame and fortune as a rock guitarist. He let his hair grow even longer, and tried his hand in Texas and in California at playing the guitar professionally.

A few years after leaving Tyler, he wrote and recorded a couple of his own songs, including one that reputedly refers to Roden. It was titled, "There's a Madman in Waco." The time would come when adversaries and critics would point to the title and lyrics as being eerily appropriate to his own behavior.

Stories eventually surfaced years later from people who had known Howell during the early 1980s that he fiddled around with mind-altering drugs, although the accusations were never confirmed. But there was no question that he was showing disturbing signs of runaway religious fanaticism. Ginger Fry, whose husband Ed was a schoolmate of Howell's in Dallas, was later quoted in *USA Today* about an unsettling confrontation she had had with him while playing with a bluegrass band.

She said Howell came backstage during intermission and began reading her the riot act, "practically calling me a whore because I was wearing blue jeans." He accused her and her husband of playing the devil's music, she said.

By the early 1980s, Howell was firmly set on the spiritual path that was to lead him and his followers to their personal Armageddon. He had not only broken most of his ties with the Seventh-Day Adventist Church, but apparently he had also virtually given up on his aspirations to become a rock music star. He moved into Mount Carmel and became a Branch Davidian. The peace-loving religious community he found there and the faith they espoused would never be the same again.

With George Roden out of the way and no church elders to disfellowship him, Howell had open sailing to reshape Mount Carmel and restructure the belief system of its occupants. While the faithful busied themselves with fix-up activities at the compound, the new Living Prophet enforced stringent rules of behavior for the community.

The Branch Davidians arose before daylight, or for a few weeks during the longer days of summer just as the first faint streaks of light were brushing the sky. Their meals were vegetarian and meager, with no frills. Typical breakfasts were cereal and a small amount of fruit. Lunch was usually a modest salad. Dinner might be popcorn and peanuts. Sometimes the Branch Davidians were permitted to eat nothing at all but peanuts. At other times Howell would boggle his skinny disciples with rapidly changing dietary rules, first decreeing that they could eat only certain fruits together, then suddenly switching the combination. The occupants of the commune were also frequently required to fast.

Separate dormitories were established for single adult males, for females, and for children.

Howell lectured and preached, and he and a few senior members of the community conducted daily Bible studies. He was an enthusiastic preacher who was long-winded enough on the pulpit to give Fidel Castro and Jessie Jackson a serious run for their money. And he often used his preaching and Bible study to test the devotion and obedience of his followers.

Sometimes after they had worked and studied until late in the evening and he was still fresh and full of energy from lying in bed until mid-afternoon, he would suddenly summon everyone for a religious lecture. Often it was just about the time they were looking forward to a Spartan late-evening meal. It wasn't uncommon, during his impromptu sermon, for him to snack on ice cream or some other treat permitted only for him.

Members of his flock would have no choice, however, except to sit and quietly listen while he confidently pranced through some of the thorniest possible theological thickets. He rambled on about such matters of deep spiritual concern as rewards for the righteous, terrible retribution for hypocrites—especially those of the Seventh-Day Adventist Church—and the Living Prophet's revealed messages from the Scriptures.

One night he might keep his bleary-eyed acolytes awake with profound revelations about the wavesheaf. The Bible speaks of the wavesheaf as the grain waved before the Lord at the beginning of the harvest. According to the Branch Davidians, however, the wavesheaf is composed of the Lord's elite. They are the courageous, faithful souls who are promoted to heaven even before the 144,000 pure and deserving destined to reign with Christ during the millennium. Leaders of messianic cults commonly use prophecy to keep members in line by warning that only the most devout and faithful will be saved.

Exhausted and hungry, the weary Branch Davidians fought to stay awake as they were told how the wavesheaf will help teach the 144,000 left behind, heal the sick, even raise the dead. The wavesheaf are special souls who must earn their exalted status through suffering, martyrdom, or other tribulations, they were taught.

The next night the Living Prophet might serenade his captive audience with a barrage of revelations from his own dreadful surrealistic visions of the Apocalypse and the millennium. His staccato hellfire-and-brimstone pulpit thumping could run fifteen hours, punctuated every now and then by his own wild shrieks mimicking the suffering of lost, tortured souls.

Howell often asked perplexing rhetorical questions that left his captive audience floundering and hesitant to even venture a try at an answer, according to former members. His lectures and discussions could be difficult to follow, even for some of his longtime disciples. At other times he would veer off the subject and begin holding forth on world affairs or science.

He wouldn't put up with any questioning of his knowledge or rightful authority. Even if someone had complained that he wasn't setting a good example, he had the answer all ready. From the first he had acknowledged serious flaws in his spiritual character. The first Messiah had been without sin. But because the new Messiah was a sinner, he was a more capable judge of good and evil, Howell declared. The new Messiah ate meat, drank beer, cursed, lusted after women, and generally indulged himself. But he didn't hesitate to judge others, and his punishment was rapid and severe.

He ejected one weak acolyte from Mount Carmel for eating a chocolate chip ice-cream cone, according to a onetime follower who later left the cult. And when he was still encamped in the boondocks at the edge of Palestine, a family was banished when he learned during a routine search of their quarters that they had been to town and bought some french fries. He never hesitated to show his power and authority.

Yet at other times, he took a handpicked favorite or two along with him on trips outside the compound to attend gun shows, or to a club, or to a nice restaurant and bar like the Chelsea Street Pub in the Richmond Mall. Despite his Texas roots, he preferred the comfortable restaurant, which served British beer, to local honky-tonks where boot-scooters in denims and cowboy hats shuffled around a dance floor while the jukebox played Willie Nelson and Waylon Jennings tunes. Once, shortly before the face-off at the compound with the ATF, the Living Prophet and a couple of companions meandered into the pub and nibbled on bean and cheese nachos and sipped ice tea while listening to a live band.

Every so often the guru from Mount Carmel

would show up at the Lone Star Music and Sound Company in Waco to shop. When he decided to buy a guitar, he always tried to drive a hard bargain, wheedling and dickering over the price. Eventually he bought thousands of dollars' worth of guitars, amplifiers, and other equipment at Lone Star and other stores in Texas and California.

He even helped a couple of the young musicians living at Mount Carmel form a rock band in Waco. They called themselves Blind Wolfe. Koresh reportedly watched them play for audiences, and he watched them practice in Waco and elsewhere, including a club in Dallas called On The Rocks.

Many of the Branch Davidians worked outside Mount Carmel. Douglas Wayne Martin lived in the compound and worked in Waco, where he was highly regarded among his professional peers. The forty-two-year-old black attorney was a computer expert, who frequently busied himself during free time with shortwave radios and other electronic equipment. His wife, Sheila Judith Martin, had moved into the commune with him and their children.

Several women from the compound had jobs as nurses at area hospitals, including the Providence Health Center. They didn't talk much at work about their personal or spiritual lives, but other nurses had the impression that they turned over most of their earnings to the cult. Others worked at a variety of both blue-collar and white-collar jobs. Peter Hipsman, a handsome bachelor from Monroe, New York, who had roamed around the country working variously as a waiter, printer, welder, and painter, had wound up working as a mechanic.

After Howell became the Living Prophet, most Branch Davidians began giving all, or almost all, of their income to the cult. Some of the older members who lived on Social Security and pensions simply turned over their monthly paychecks. According to high-ranking ATF investigators, many members gave everything they owned after joining the cult, selling their homes and personal property, then turning over the money to Howell. Simple tithing of 10 percent reportedly fell by the wayside for most Branch Davidians living in the compound after the new leader took charge.

The Branch Davidians set up several businesses, according to local and state government authorities. The Branch Organic Agricultural Association was one. The Universal Publishing Association, and Living Waters were others.

Neighbors who lived in nearby Elk or on the ranches and farms of McLennan County became used to seeing the men and women they sometimes referred to as Carmelites riding about in pickup trucks and on go-carts or Harley-Davidsons. The Branch Davidians even bought jet skis to use on the Trading House Creek Reservoir or on other local waterways. They were polite, well behaved, and they minded their own business—a trait especially treasured by many rural Texans. Despite the gunplay at Mount Carmel during the dispute over leadership, most neighbors considered the Branch Davidians to be simply clannish members of a religious commune, not dangerous cultists.

Walter Dulock, operator of The Elk Store, an old-fashioned general store, and a resident of the little town near the compound since 1934, got along well with his curious neighbors from Mount Carmel. They dropped by the store every once in a while to buy gasoline, candy, soft drinks or other odds and ends.

Often members of the religious commune made much larger purchases from local merchants. And they sometimes peddled honey produced by the bees they tended. The men looked pretty much like any of the other farmers or tradesmen around the area. The women were more conspicuous because of their long skirts, buttoned-up blouses, and lack of makeup.

Children from Mount Carmel attended classes at schools in the town of Axtell off and on for years. They would attend public school classes for a while, then they would be withdrawn and taught at the compound by Branch Davidians who were teachers. After a few months or a year or two, however, they would return to the public schools. Their fitful presence at the Axtell schools continued until about 1991, when eleven boys and girls were withdrawn for good, to be taught at Mount Carmel.

But when they were attending public schools they were well behaved. Some were outstanding students, and one boy who was especially good in science and math won district contests. Branch Davidian children didn't sleep over or attend birthday parties at the houses of their schoolmates. No birthday parties were held at the commune, either. And children from outside hadn't stayed overnight at Mount Carmel since the 1960s or early 1970s, when the Rodens were in charge. The longer Howell headed the group, the more clannish it became.

In 1990 Vernon Howell became David Koresh. He filed a petition in California State Superior Court in Pomona on May 15 to legally change his name, and on August 28 the petition was granted by Judge Robert Martinez. The cult leader stated on the legal documents that he was an entertainer and desired the name change for publicity and business purposes.

*Koresh* is Hebrew for "Cyrus" and was linked by the former Vernon Howell and others to Cyrus the Great, founder of the Persian Empire. Koresh was also the surname of God, the cult leader said. And it could also mean "death."

The ex-husband of one of Koresh's followers, who himself was never a cult member, later claimed to a television talk-show host that the Branch Davidians believed David would be the name of Christ when the Messiah returned. Thus, the name David Koresh could be interpreted as "Christ the destroyer of Babylon." God is also said to have promised the biblical King David that one of his descendants would one day rule a heavenly kingdom.

After the final leadership change at the compound, some neighbors, and reportedly some of the people at Mount Carmel, began to refer to the cultists not as Branch Davidians, but as Koreshians.

Howell's adoption of the name didn't mark the first time that the name Koresh has been used by a captivating spiritual leader. In 1870 Cyrus Read Teed, an unorthodox former corporal in the Union army medical corps, proclaimed himself to be the seventh messenger of God and adopted Koresh as his new surname.

He explained that an angel had visited him and provided guidance on his new spiritual path. The early Koresh said he was the reincarnated Messiah and it was his job to gather the 144,000 worthy to await the Last Judgment. He taught that God was both male and female.

Along with his religious beliefs, the nineteenth-century Koresh also taught a revolutionary concept of the universe with the mind-warping name "cellular cosmogony." We aren't living on the outside of the earth, he believed, but exist on the inside of a hollow sphere with a floating sun that is half dark and half light and only appears to be rising and setting. He was so convinced of the truth of his theory that he offered ten thousand dollars, a staggering amount of money at that time, to anyone who could disprove it. No one collected the money, although some scientists and mathematicians tried.

Teed abandoned everything that had previously been important to him to teach his revolutionary theory of the universe and to follow his new spiritual path. A thriving medical practice he had built up as an herbalist, as well as a wife and child, were left behind.

The first Koresh was born in New York State. He grew up on a farm but moved to the Midwest before he began attracting a signficant following. Koresh set up his first religious commune in

Chicago and began publishing a magazine called the *Flaming Sword*, to help spread his message. Like the later Koresh, he was a captivating lecturer and attracted scores of disciples. Many women abandoned husbands and children to follow him.

Around the turn of the century he purchased a three-hundred-acre tract in a rural area of Florida near Fort Myers to establish the "New Jerusalem." He called the settlement the Koreshan Unity, Inc.

But the Messenger's dreams eluded him, and most of his energy during his unhappy years in Florida was wasted in quarrels with his neighbors, local government officials, and police. After his death in a boating accident in 1908, his followers waited in vain for his resurrection. After four days, county health authorities forced them to bury him. The early Koresh was laid to rest in a mausoleum on the Fort Myers beach and was guarded around the clock by his loyal disciples. In 1921 it was washed away by a hurricane.

A few believers continued to follow the teachings of the onetime herbalist until the early 1980s, when the last of the Florida-based Koreshians died.

By the time Vernon Howell changed his name, he was already making regular references to himself as the Lamb of God, which is spoken of in Revelation. Many fundamentalists believe the Lamb is another name for Christ. Eventual defectors from the cult claimed that Howell agreed with that definition, and considered himself to be Christ.

He had new calling cards printed. The word "Messiah" was centered on the front of the cards in thick, black, inch-high type. The *i* in "Messiah" was dotted with a star, and the drawing of a sword made a dramatic slash through the name.

Koresh mixed religion and business on the heavy gold-colored cards, which were also imprinted just under "Messiah" with "Cyrus Productions." At the very bottom were the business titles and names of himself and his chief lieutenant: "David Koresh: Guitar, Vocals" and "Steve Schneider: Music Manager."

There were no addresses or telephone numbers on the card, although Koresh made sure he got his money's worth by listing nine Bible verses on the back. One of the verses was from Revelation.

As the Messiah, Christ, or the Living Prophet, defectors and the lapsed faithful began warning, he was prepared to lead his flock to doomsday and beyond.

\* \* \*

After the acquittals and mistrial following the shootout with Roden, attorney Gary Coker, Jr., drove back to Mount Carmel with five semiautomatic rifles, a pair of shotguns, and twenty-nine hundred rounds of ammunition the sheriff's deputies had confiscated. The lawyer said his clients had bought the guns at a local K-Mart before the shootout.

The weapons, all legal under Texas and United States laws regulating possession and use of firearms, became the nucleus for a formidable arsenal put together by the winners of the power struggle. It was an arms collection that could be used to defend against an attack by disaffected dropouts—or by far more consequential enemies.

The Living Prophet began adding to the cache with more powerful and rapid-fire weapons and accoutrements purchased at gun shows, area firearms supply stores, and by mail order from suppliers as far away as South Carolina. Some of the sophisticated firearms he purchased were reportedly capable of hitting targets a mile away.

A few years after Koresh assumed total control at Mount Carmel, federal authorities developed intelligence leading them to believe that the cultists were designing and preparing to manufacture their own crude submachine guns. Investigators learned that a member of the commune was a mechanical engineer, thought to be using a computer to work out the design of the illegal "grease gun." The cultists had their own metal lathe and milling machinery.

The armory was set up next to the chapel, and Koresh kept the key. Weapons and ammunition were issued to members for target practice sessions and when they had guard duty at the gate or on the tower. Neighbors were used to hearing gunfire coming from the woods and scrub-brush pastureland surrounding the compound.

While putting together the arsenal, the cultists also installed a thousand-gallon propane tank and purchased and stored hundreds of pounds of millet and pinto beans, dozens of cartons of canned goods, powdered milk, and thousands of "Meals, Ready-to-Eat," the same MREs used by the military during Operation Desert Storm. A good portion of the supplies were paid for in part with food stamps turned over to the cult by elderly and female members.

The doomsday preparations mirrored, in some respects, the preparations of many American families who constructed or purchased bomb shelters during the 1950s and 1960s in anticipation of a nuclear attack. The bunkers of thirty and forty years ago were stocked with food; then the owners bought guns to defend themselves from unprepared neighbors when the expected holocaust occurred.

The Branch Davidians, of course, weren't the first apocalyptic cultists to prepare to defend themselves from anticipated attacks by frightened, desperate unbelievers during the End Times.

Charlie Manson, the career convict and renegade Pied Piper who led a ragtag collection of hippies to commit some of the most notorious murders of the century, lured his followers with a message that has curious similarities to belief in the Rapture and the Apocalypse. Convinced that he was picking up secret messages from the music of the Beatles, Manson was accused of directing the murders of actress Sharon Tate and others in order to set off a deadly race war the clan referred to as Helter-Skelter.

Drawing on old Hopi Indian legends about a hole in the desert leading to middle-earth, Manson reportedly planned to lead his Family to a safe refuge, there to wait out the holocaust. Blacks were expected to win, but their victory would be flawed because they would be left without the superior intelligence of the whites. That was when Manson would emerge from the cave with his band of drugged-out hippies, the last living white people, and rule during a new golden age on earth. Curiously, Manson was also a frustrated musician who had sought his professional breakthrough in southern California.

As with the mixed-up flower children who followed Manson, somewhere along the way the Davidian message of love and peace had gotten lost. The message of spiritual redemption that had marked most of the history of the Branch Davidians, and of the Seventh-Day Adventists from which they splintered, was becoming hopelessly tangled and twisted. Koresh was fusing AK-47s and the Prince of Peace in the minds of himself and his followers.

When he wasn't preaching about the Apocalypse, the Rambo Messiah played videos of violent films based on the Vietnam War for his followers, who were normally banned from watching television or movies. His favorite actor was Jean-Claude Van Damme, and *Platoon*, *Full Metal Jacket*, and *Hamburger Hill* were some of his choice films. He played them over and over. The films might appear to be curious fare for onetime professed pacifists, but they provided important psychological conditioning for the coming tribulations.

Koresh's warnings, issued during Bible classes and in conversations with individuals or with small groups, that the final battle with the Philistines was rapidly approaching grew increasingly strident and desperate. Devoted members of his flock became convinced that sacrifice and martyrdom were not to be feared, and instead could elevate one of the devout to a place among the wavesheaf.

James Tom, an Australian who eventually defected, later recalled the day when Koresh demanded to know, "How far are you prepared to go?" According to the report in *Time* magazine, when his bewildered acolyte hesitated, the Living Prophet made the question crystal clear with a dreadful elaboration: "Which of your two children are you prepared to sacrifice?" he asked.

Koresh's biblical convictions about Armageddon became a bewilderingly combustible mush of religious fanaticism, secular survivalism. and paranoia. The commune was preparing for a siege and the final battle between good and evil that would lead to the millennium, God's Kingdom on Earth.

While he taught his followers, Koresh continued his own detailed scrutiny and philosophical dissection of ecclesiastical fine points in the Bible. The only prophetic book of the New Testament, which some people know as Revelation and others refer to as the Apocalypse of John, as always drew special attention while he sought to understand the sometimes obscure and confusing allegories, metaphors, and dark visions of the intermediate chapters.

His fervent studies and dour musings apparently led him to announce to his dutiful flock that he would be endowed with divine power to open the final and dreadful seventh seal spoken of in Revelation and bring on the horrors of hell on earth. Only then, after devastating plagues and cataclysms had rolled over the earth, would Jesus return to lead his followers in Armageddon, the final battle against evil.

Many fundamentalist Christians believe the Lamb of God to be Jesus himself, and that only he can break the seals that will set off the cataclysms and lead to God's Kingdom on Earth. The inference was obvious. If Koresh could break the seals, then he was Jesus Christ reincarnated.

Koresh believed himself to be the hero of the Great Tribulation spoken of in Revelation 5. The chapter says in part: "Then one of the elders said to me, 'Do not weep! See, the Lion of the tribe of Judah, the Root of David, has triumphed. He is able to open the scroll and its seven seals.' "

The first four seals of Revelation are represented by the mounts of the Four Horsemen of the Apocalypse: a white horse symbolizing evil or imperialism; the red horse of war; the black horse of famine; and the pale horse of death. The fifth seal is equated with suffering and a demand for vengeance from martyred souls; the sixth seal is believed to be symbolic of natural calamities such as cataclysmic solar eclipses, meteor collisions with the earth, tidal waves, earthquakes, volcanic eruptions, killer storms, and a devastating war involving two hundred million soldiers.

Cult defectors later claimed they were taught to think of themselves as God's marines. If they couldn't die for God, they couldn't live for God.

At last, Mount Carmel was given a new name. The Koreshians began calling their settlement Ranch Apocalypse. And, defectors would eventually claim, some began preparing themselves for martyrdom in the final world-shaking battle.

# CHAPTER FIVE

# The House of David

WHILE KORESH WAS BRINGING CATACLYS-
mic changes to life inside Mount Carmel, he was
also strengthening his hold on his followers and
beating the bushes for new recruits.

He looked in Texas, California, Hawaii, Canada, Israel, England, Australia, New Zealand,
and the Caribbean, anywhere he might find converts. He approached prospects in restaurants,
nightclubs, and in their homes. He even used his
skill as a rock musician and his musical colleagues to lure newcomers to the cult. Koresh

personally buttonholed other musicians and urged them to return with him to Texas and play for the Lord.

Singer Sheridan Stewart was treated to one of his seductive recruiting sales jobs in a Los Angeles rock music club. Sprinkling his spiel with biblical references, he attempted to woo the long-haired beauty by telling her he believed in giving women more of an active role in religious life. He was impressive, but she wasn't buying. She later told *People* magazine she didn't want to sing in a band with a man who thought he was Jesus.

But David Thibodeaux wasn't as dubious after meeting up with the cult leader in a Los Angeles music supply store. The young drummer was hooked through his love of music and his desire for a change from the neon sinfulness of Los Angeles nightclubs and life in the fast lane. He was looking for a more spiritual existence with the Branch Davidians, according to his mother, Balinda Ganem. Months after her son joined the cult, Mrs. Ganem said during an interview on *The Oprah Winfrey Show* that he was offered a full-time job with a band and an opportunity to study the Bible with a teacher who had vast spiritual insight.

"He was very impressed," the Bangor, Maine, woman said of her son's reading of the cult leader. "There was a charismatic, electrifying personality."

Jaime Castillo, another handsome drummer, was lured into the cult in much the same way. The young El Monte, California man joined the Branch Davidians in 1991 and played in the cult leader's rock group.

Despite his occasional success enlisting young people like Thibodeaux and Castillo, Koresh had even more fertile sources of potential recruits. He worked hard to bring former supporters of Benjamin and Lois Roden back to the fold. But he especially preyed on other splinter Davidian groups and on Seventh-Day Adventists wherever he found them, in local church congregations or at parochial schools and colleges.

He even enlisted his mother, but she eventually left the cult. Nevertheless, she continued to be impressed by her son. Years after leaving the cult, she conceded that although she didn't agree with everything he did, she still wanted to believe God was working through him.

Although there were vast differences between his breakaway sect and the conservative, mainline Protestant denomination it had ultimately sprung from, the common belief in the Second Advent and the End Times provided him with a powerful foothold to use in his proselytizing. Adventists tended to give the zealous young missionary an opportunity to make his case. Some Adventists managed to maintain a dual loyalty, attending services and tithing with their regular church congregation, and contributing money and sharing in Bible study and other activities with the Branch Davidians as well.

Koresh's father-in-law found Marc Breault stocking groceries at a store near the campus of Loma Linda University, a Seventh-Day Adventist–affiliated school several miles east of Los Angeles. Perry Jones was recruiting and used the Dallas Cowboys T-shirt Breault was wearing as an excuse to open a conversation. Jones told the serious, curly-haired twenty-two-year-old that he was from Texas. He also told him about David Koresh and the Branch Davidians.

Breault, who was born into the Roman Catholic Church, had been a teenager attending a church camp for the vision impaired when he switched his religious allegiances to the Seventh-Day Adventists. Nearly blind, with only 5 percent vision in his left eye, he had studied at the church-affiliated school in Loma Linda for the ministry and was working on a master's degree in religion.

The timing of the meeting was terrible for Breault and nearly perfect for Koresh, according to the former theological student's later account on television's popular *Donahue* show. Breault said he basically had been advised that there was no room in the church for a blind pastor. After investing four years and a large amount of money in an education that had left him without a career, the young man was especially vulnerable when he had his fateful meeting with Jones and the Living Prophet.

Koresh quickly wooed Breault into the cult, promising an opportunity to mix the ministry with music. The enthusiastic recruit would play keyboard in Koresh's rock and roll band, even though Koresh's big plans to win converts with music eventually fizzled. The young people attracted to rock and roll ultimately wanted good times, not doomsday preaching about the impending end of the world.

Breault traveled back to Texas with his new mentor, where the breakaway Branch Davidians were still living near Palestine. Like Robyn Bunds, he had a lot of adjusting to do. The uninviting packing boxes, tents, and scrub brush around Palestine, Texas, was separated from California, and from Hawaii where Breault had previously lived, by much more than mere geographical distance.

But despite the primitive living conditions at Palestine, and later at Mount Carmel, Koresh and his followers were good at rustling members and students from Seventh-Day Adventist churches and schools. Seventh-Day Adventist leaders, of course, did whatever they could to resist Koresh's parasitic poaching.

At the Southwestern Adventist College in Keene, Texas, along U.S. Highway 67 about fifty miles south of Fort Worth, police were sometimes called to eject Branch Davidian proselytizers attempting to pass out religious tracts in the library and in residential halls. At other times elders complained that Branch Davidians would come to church, begin passing out literature, then begin shouting, quarreling, and trying to take over the services.

Despite reported complaints from some college officials, however, the cult's recruiters were permitted to distribute their literature during the annual camp meetings in May or June. The camp meetings are open to the public and Keene police were reluctant to do anything that might get them entangled in a legal hassle over First Amendment rights.

But just about everybody in the little college town of approximately four thousand people attends the Seventh-Day Adventist Church. And the nine hundred Adventist students at the liberal arts college were prime targets of Koresh's messianic missionaries.

Police were also called to oust Branch Davidians trying to lure members away from the Grace

Temple Seventh-Day Adventist Church in Fort Worth. Seven or eight men and women who had begun attending the church's services and religious classes were kicked out after they began preaching cult dogma and handing out religious tracts.

Koresh twice traveled to Israel to spread his message, after informing his disciples that when he began to convert the Jews the world would be thrown into turmoil. Armageddon would begin when American troops finally invaded the Holy Land, and he would be changed into an avenging angel who would smite down the wicked in preparation for the new heavenly kingdom on earth, he reportedly told the faithful.

He first visited the Holy Land in 1985, and then again five years later, each time walking the ancient streets of Jerusalem. He visited the Wailing Wall, retraced the path along the Via Dolorosa where Christ walked to the Crucifixion, and trekked to the Garden of Gethsemane where Jesus suffered his agony, betrayal, and arrest; and always, Koresh evangelized. But there was no rush among the Israelis to join the fast-talking cult leader from America.

The Jews in Jerusalem and in other cities and towns or communes throughout Israel had already heard from a regular procession of deluded or mad prophets and holy men who believed they were the reincarnated Messiah, King David, Abraham, Moses, or John the Baptist. The slender, intense, silver-tongued Texan who called himself the Living Prophet was nothing special to become concerned about.

He had better luck in Hawaii and in England.

Paul Fatta was living in Hawaii when the Living Prophet swept into Honolulu on a recruiting swing. The son of a retired air force sergeant and Catholic high school graduate, he had already become interested in the Seventh-Day Adventist Church when he was first exposed to David Koresh's inspired Bible lectures.

Steve and Judy Schneider were two other important recruits Koresh found in Hawaii. Steve Schneider was a graduate of the University of Hawaii with a bachelor's degree in religion. He became one of Koresh's closest confidants, both for the Living Prophet's musical career and, more important, in affairs related to the internal workings of the cult. His wife, Judy, became one of the leading and most authoritative female members of the Branch Davidians.

The Schneiders, Fatta, and about a dozen other people moved from Hawaii to the compound in the isolated scrubland and cow pastures of central Texas.

One elderly couple from Hawaii wound up turning over about half a million dollars to the religious community. Fatta turned over about fifty thousand dollars in musical equipment and vehicles to the cult. But he later told a reporter that the property still belonged to him and he could take it back if he wished.

Steve Schneider accompanied Koresh during a whirlwind trip to England in 1988. The Living Prophet picked up some of his most valuable recruits at the Adventists' Newbold College near the town of Bracknell, and he raided or attempted to raid Seventh-Day Adventist congregations in London, Manchester, Birmingham, and Nottingham.

Koresh, who was still using his birth name, mined the college, which is about a half-hour drive from London, for converts during a stopover of a few days. The more impressionable among the theological students were entranced by the messianic young lecturer. Alternately shouting, wheedling, and making promises of divine favor, Koresh spouted bits and pieces of the Scriptures in his distinctive Texas drawl for hours until his audience was exhausted.

Dr. Hugh Dunton, a regular lecturer at the college, later told news reporters that the visiting preacher gave the impression during the rambling speech that he was semidivine—and would probably kill if he believed it would help mankind. In a formal statement released by

Newbold College, Dr. Dunton said Koresh had deep-rooted problems. "In addition to the claims he was making for himself," the college spokesman further observed, "he had an obvious obsession with sex."

Three students studying at the college for the ministry were nevertheless so taken with Koresh's charisma and entranced with the power of his message that they were quickly enlisted as converts. The recruits, along with Koresh, reportedly sometimes referred to themselves as "the four beasts of the Book of Revelation."

Livingston Fagan, a small black man in his early thirties, was a member of the quartet, and he quickly became entangled in disputes with more conventional members of the church and college faculty. The congregation complained about his sermons, and he authored a religious tract that Dr. Dunton later described as "pretty incomprehensible."

"Livingston was preying on new converts, ultras and people looking for an experience beyond what they already had," the theologian told the *Evening Standard.*

Fagan, who was a member of the Nottingham Seventh-Day Adventist Church with his wife, Yvette, and two children, Renee and Neharah, defected to Koresh and became one of his most devoted and successful recruiters. His former minister described him as a headstrong man who deviated from their teachings and was a ringleader in influencing and recruiting younger members of the congregation.

Pastor Eric Lowe of the Nottingham church cautioned members of his congregation who were approached by Fagan or other recruiters that the American cult leader might be another Jim Jones. The Reverend Jones, a onetime Indiana clergyman, was head of a cult called the People's Temple. He shocked people around the world on November 18, 1978, by leading nine hundred of his followers in an orgy of mass suicide and murder in Guyana. Most of them died when they drank arsenic-laced Kool-Aid.

Despite the Reverend Lowe's concern and his efforts to protect his flock, there were other defectors from the congregation. Winston Blake, a gentle man with the burly build of a National Football League linebacker, a fondness for Indian curry, a love of the Bible, and a deep concern for his spiritual life, joined the pilgrimage to Mount Carmel after his girlfriend was recruited. Beverly Elliott was a computer graphics artist from Manchester, and when she succumbed to the Branch Davidian evangelizing, Blake went along with her.

John McBean was one of the Newbold students who was impressed with the visitor from the

United States. And a little more than a year after Koresh's perturbing visit to the college, McBean's girlfriend, Diana Henry, set up a three-evening series of home Bible classes in Manchester. Steve Schneider taught the studies.

Several suspicious clergymen from local churches sat in on the classes, but they usually left before midnight. The classes continued on much longer than that, and it wasn't until after the ministers left that Schneider reportedly turned to the serious matters of trekking to the Mount of Olives to await Armageddon and other cryptic doomsday talk.

Miss Henry was recruited for the Texas-based cult shortly after graduating from college with a degree in psychology. Within a short time she drew her fifty-five-year-old mother, Zilla, two sisters, and two brothers into the cult. Mrs. Henry and her children left England for Texas. McBean also moved to Mount Carmel.

The only member of the once-cohesive Manchester family who refused to join the mass religious defection was Zilla Henry's husband, Samuel. The heartbroken construction worker eventually traveled to Waco for a showdown with Koresh in a desperate effort to get his family back. But when he returned to England it was without his wife and children. His marriage of twenty-eight years wound up in divorce.

Koresh eventually lured about a dozen converts away from Manchester churches. Most, although not all, were young college-educated men and women. Twenty-seven-year-old Norman Washington Allison was a factory worker when he pulled up stakes and headed for the United States and a hardscrabble life in the central Texas boondocks. Almost all the recruits from the United Kingdom were black, and many were either immigrants, or the children of immigrants, from Jamaica.

When twenty-six-year-old Sandra Hardial joined up with the cult she had a good job with the City Council's housing department in the industrial town of a half-million northwest of London. A college graduate and athletic woman who bowled and regularly trekked to the Swiss Alps to ski, she and several other interested men and women from Manchester first spent a couple of weeks at Mount Carmel taking Bible study and meeting members of the commune.

But she had resumed her job in Manchester and several months later was expected to join her parents and only brother on a vacation in Jamaica, when she failed to show up. When they got back to England they found a note from her saying she was returning to Texas to live with the Branch Davidians.

A few years later a high-ranking FBI official

described the typical people he believed Koresh targeted as potential recruits. "He looks for the lonely, the lost, the unloved, the innocent," said Special Agent Bob Ricks. "These are the people he has brought into his fold, who will do anything that he orders them to do."

Complying with some of the professed Messiah's orders could lead to heart-wrenching decisions that put the loyalty and faith of his followers to the acid test.

The Living Prophet's revelation about the "New Light" created more anguish among his flock than any other event prior to the shootout with the ATF. Not even the disturbing buildup of weapons and the move to armed militancy among the former pacifist cultists had led to so much serious doubt and disillusionment with the rapidly mutating Branch Davidian creed.

He was still calling himself Vernon Howell in August 1989 when he claimed the right to have any and all of the female members of the sect for his own. In fact, he reportedly declared that all the women in the world were rightfully his. He had been divinely charged with the task of creating a house of many wives, just as the biblical King David had done, he explained.

Koresh was at the house in Pomona regaling several of his male followers for a few hours with one of his monologues about the seven seals and

Armageddon when he made the startling disclosure.

The Living Prophet explained that it was all part of his mission to create an army of God's children from his own seed; their function was to share special leadership roles during the golden age of the millennium. God was lonesome. And Koresh said that as the Lamb, it was his job to provide the Deity with grandchildren. The women chosen to bear those children would live in the new House of David.

The announcement was devastating. Howell's disciples had already given up just about everything but their physical lives and their spouses. Now the men were being told that their wives, sweethearts, sisters, daughters—and mothers— were being demanded as well. The message was clear to the men and to the women: to resist would be going against the will of God.

Several formerly loyal couples left nevertheless. The runaway carnality of the arrogant megalomaniac who had seized leadership of the Branch Davidians was turning their former dreams of sharing in God's glorious kingdom into a shoddy nightmare. But most of Koresh's followers swallowed their doubts and remained. His hold on them became tighter than ever before.

Although the Book of Revelation continued to

"I am Christ": Branch Davidian leader David Koresh at age 14.
(AP/Wide World Photos)

David Koresh on video from Australia. (James Pozarik, courtesy of The Gamma Liaison Network)

Koresh in a 1981 picture taken at the Branch Davidian compound near Waco, Texas. (Courtesy of DB/SABA)

Koresh with wife Rachel and son Cyrus, approximately six years ago. (AP/Wide World Photos)

Koresh's children: son Cyrus at age six and daughter Star at age four. (AP/Wide World Photos)

Cattle graze peacefully in a field before the Branch Davidians' Mount Carmel compound near Waco. (AP/Wide World Photos)

Aerial photo taken earlier this year by the Bureau of Alcohol, Tobacco and Firearms. (AP/Wide World Photos)

On February 28, 1993 agents with the Bureau of Alcohol, Tobacco and Firearms stormed the Branch Davidian compound. The raid resulted in several deaths and marked the beginning of a 51-day standoff between cult members and law enforcement officials. (AP/Wide World Photos)

A Texas National Guard armored personnel carrier heads toward Mount Carmel just hours after the February 28th raid. (AP/Wide World Photos)

An ATF tactical operations officer looks through one of the many cameras positioned outside the Branch Davidian compound. (AP/Wide World Photos)

*(Above)* Linda Cox displays a T-shirt she is selling near the compound. During the 51-day siege, thousands of tourists flocked to Waco to observe the compound and the FBI/ATF operation set up at its perimeter. (AP/Wide World Photos) *(Right)* Texas Department of Safety officers stand by a signpost erected at a checkpoint near the Branch Davidian compound. (AP/Wide World Photos) *(Below)* Tony Suckla sits inside his car near the barricade of a road leading to the compound. Suckla, an elder in the Pleasant Grove Church of the Seventh Day Adventists in Dallas, said he was handing out religious books to passersby. (AP/Wide World Photos)

Branch Davidian member Kathy Schroeder is escorted from the federal courthouse after a hearing. (AP/Wide World Photos)

Marshals escort Livingston Fagan of England, center, being held as a material witness, and Kevin Whitecliff into the federal courthouse for a hearing. (AP/Wide World Photos)

*(Left)* A Chinook helicopter flies over the burning Mount Carmel compound. (G. Reed Schumann/Reuter, Courtesy of Bettmann) *(Above)* Fire engulfs the Branch Davidian compound after FBI agents in an armored vehicle smashed the buildings and pumped in tear gas in an effort to end the standoff. The Justice Department alleges that cult members set the fire themselves in an act of mass suicide. (AP/Wide World Photos) *(Below)* Apocalypse: An aerial view of the fire-ravaged compound taken from 8,500 feet. (AP/Wide World Photos)

receive major attention from Koresh, he began referring frequently to a phrase from the Forty-fifth Psalm, which mentions the head of the king being anointed with the oil of gladness. Koresh reportedly claimed the "oil of gladness" referred to vaginal secretions with which the wives anointed the king's penis during sexual intercourse.

Koresh also turned to the biblical King Solomon's erotic Song of Songs to further buttress his sexual claim on the women of the world. He cited a verse that says in part: "threescore queens, and fourscore concubines, and virgins without number."

And he borrowed the term "Mighty Men," who are described in the biblical story as the guards of King Solomon's bed, to bestow on his male followers. Like the Mighty Men of the Bible, the new Mighty Men would guard the bed of the new king and fight and defeat unbelievers.

Rachel and Robyn were only the first of at least fifteen Branch Davidian females that Howell-Koresh would eventually take as his own during the next few years. The unions were simple: he merely selected the female of his choice, and she became his wife when she joined him in bed.

He sometimes singled out unmarried women who were as young as or younger than his legal wife, Rachel, was when they married. Long before he announced the New Light, he boasted to his followers about a reputed command from God that he share his seed with a fourteen-year-old girl. The men and women in his Bible classes were also regaled with another story from the Living Prophet about a thirteen-year-old girl he took into his bed, a couple of former members later claimed. He said her heart was pounding so hard he could hear it.

He bragged to his captive audience about having sex for the first time with his legal wife's younger sister, Michelle, when she was about twelve years old. Former members later recalled that he thought it was funny she was frightened and struggled against him as he took her pants off.

Michelle was fourteen in February 1989 when she gave birth to her first child, a girl named Serenity Sea. Wives installed in the Living Prophet's new House of David had lots of babies. Robyn's mother, Jeannine Bunds, and sister cult members who were nurses or midwives delivered some at Mount Carmel. Others were delivered in California, and occasionally at the homes of the mothers.

Robyn and another member of the cult each traveled to California to have their babies. Robyn's son, Wisdom, was born in Pomona on November 14, 1988. Later, Robyn had her son's name changed to the more conventional Shaun.

Jeannine Bunds was kept busy bringing the fruit of the Living Prophet's seed into the world. Among others she has said she delivered were twin girls to Koresh's young sister-in-law. Except for a few of the first to be born, most of the babies had no father listed on their birth certificates. But the Branch Davidians at Mount Carmel all knew who the father was.

Howell, then Koresh, didn't prey only on adolescents and other single females. He also selected mature women who were already married to some of his most loyal male followers. The cult leader simply declared that all other marriages were annulled. Marc Breault had been married to his Australian bride, Elizabeth Baranyai, for three months when Koresh made his surprise announcement about the New Light.

The Living Prophet made an audiotape of the line of religious mumbo jumbo he used to explain the New Light. And he sent a copy to some Branch Davidians from Australia to cement his hold on them or to lure them back to the fold now that they had returned home. In the tape, which became known as *The Foundation*, he explained that only the Lamb's seed could establish the House of David.

"There's only one hard-on in this whole universe that really loves you and wants to say good things about you," he advised female listeners to the tape.

Koresh was in Melbourne, Australia, regaling Branch Davidians and prospective recruits with stories of his divine mission, when Nicole Gent returned home from college. Howell had been preaching to her father, Bruce, and her stepmother, Lisa, when the nineteen-year-old coed returned home and was included in the exhausting round of marathon monologues and Bible studies.

Although she hadn't cared much for the egotistical Texan before her return home from college, one night after enduring four days of almost nonstop evangelizing she walked into her parents' bedroom and made a shocking announcement. Vernon wanted her to be his "teddy bear" that night, and she wanted their approval.

By that time the elder Gents had been brainwashed into believing their glib houseguest's claims that he had a divine purpose to provide God with grandchildren. Convinced that Nicole had been blessed by a holy call to the House of David, they gave their consent.

When Koresh returned to Mount Carmel, Nicole went with him and was installed as one of the favorites in his harem. About a year later she returned to Australia to give birth to her first child, Dayland. Her twin, Peter, was one of the Branch Davidians later killed in the shootout with the government agents.

The Living Prophet gradually chipped away at the contact between the cult's males and females. They ate separately, and they lived separate lives. Eventually, even cultists who had been husband and wife were unable to spend hardly any time with each other except during Bible studies. Koresh severely scolded them if he caught them trying to maintain contact with each other.

Eliminating the close relationship that exists in marriage is a classic ploy, according to experts who have studied cults and deprogrammed former members. Separated from their life partner, husbands and wives lose their closest confidants and consequently are dependent more than ever before on the guidance and authority of their religious or political guru.

Koresh explained to his disciples that males were naturally sexually aroused if they were around females, and the new rules were for their own good. During one Bible class, he ordered one of the young women to raise her dress and show her panties. After she complied he polled the men about whether or not most of them were sexually excited by the display. Almost all of them raised their hands.

That was proof, Koresh pointed out, that it was best to keep the sexes separated. The Lamb seemed to enjoy talking during his Bible classes about his sexual romps and specific acts he engaged in with various wives. He regaled the study groups with the sex talk while the wives, legal husbands, and their children were present.

Incredibly, sometimes when Koresh was discussing the matter with male cultists he portrayed himself as the one who deserved the sympathy. After all, his wives didn't have perfect bodies or they were imperfect in other ways, he pointed out. But as the chosen one, the Lamb, it was his cross to bear.

Koresh promised the disappointed men, who were sworn to celibacy, that they would be rewarded in the new heavenly kingdom. Each man was promised that, like Adam, he would have a wife fashioned for him from his own rib. And that wife would be the perfect mate, since she was fashioned from his own body.

That wasn't good enough for burly Winston Blake of Nottingham. He was disillusioned and told his brother-in-law during a telephone chat that his marriage plans had been called off. The cult leader had his eye on Blake's girlfriend for the harem. The big man, who loved cooking and home decorating, wanted to return to England, but Koresh wouldn't permit it.

The Branch Davidians bought another two-story house in the quaint college town of La Verne, California, at the southern edge of the Los Angeles National Forest. Koresh set aside a dormitory in the white stucco building as special quarters for eighteen wives. Male followers, when they were in California, stayed in the Pomona house. But alarmed neighbors in La Verne eventually went to child welfare authorities and complained that one of the wives was only twelve years old. The subsequent investigation of possible child molestation was still under way when the armed clash with the ATF occurred at Mount Carmel.

Despite the outrageous sales job, not everyone among the Branch Davidians automatically accepted the startling new doctrine. Some men broke down in tears. A former member of the cult later said that Livingston Fagan was one of the quicker members of Koresh's inner circle to speak up against the idea. And the little recruiter from Nottingham lost favor with Koresh as a result.

Robyn was already unhappy with the idea of sharing Koresh with other women; then Koresh swept her fifty-year-old mother into the House of David. He promised Jeannine Bunds that, like so many of the other women, she would become pregnant and bear one of God's grandchildren.

Jeannine, who worked as a nurse at the Providence Health Center in Waco, had been married for twenty-five years. She and her husband were troubled by the command and talked earnestly about the implications, but ultimately they concluded that they had to obey. And Jeannine was pleased to be selected for the House of David, where she could bear a child for the Lord.

Moving into the House of David not only separated her from her husband, it also had the effect of virtually isolating her from her daughter. The cult leader forbade the mother and daughter to talk to each other. The order was typical of the behavior of cult leaders, who often separate family members from each other in order to make them more dependent on the authority of the guru or the group.

Jim Jones used similar techniques, breaking up families soon after they were recruited into the People's Temple. Married couples were separated and children were given to other members to raise. Jones demanded all allegiance and authority—as well as any of the cult's women he desired—for himself.

Mrs. Bunds later talked on *Oprah* about the New Light and her induction into the House of David. It made sense to her, she said, "because he would start with Psalm Forty-five and he would go into the seven seals and he would go into Revelation. He had a whole Bible study." Koresh was very good at quoting Scripture, she said.

Koresh was doing what he had always done since moving into Mount Carmel during the shaky leadership reign of Lois Roden. He was picking and choosing elements of the Scriptures that suited his purposes and ignoring or twisting the rest.

By the time Jeannine Bunds joined the House of David, her daughter also knew a lot about Scripture. Robyn had spent much of her life studying the Bible, and Revelation, Daniel, and Elijah weren't the only books she was familiar with. One of the Old Testament books she knew a lot about was Leviticus. And she knew that Levitical law forbids a man to be the lover of a woman and her daughter, or of a woman and her granddaughter.

Robyn was becoming fed up with the Living Prophet's sexual shenanigans and other questionable behavior. She wasn't alone. Marc Breault, Elizabeth Baranyai, and others were doing some painful questioning of Koresh's motives and behavior as well.

# CHAPTER SIX

# Defectors

IT WAS INEVITABLE THAT SOME OF THE
Branch Davidians would ultimately become fed
up with the shenanigans at Mount Carmel and
refuse to settle anymore for Koresh's heavenly
IOUs.

Marc Breault knew that Koresh had gone too
far when the cult leader announced the New
Light.

But it wasn't only himself and his bride he was
concerned about. The former divinity student
simply couldn't excuse Koresh's focus on young

girls as sexual prey. And that had been going on long before the silver-tongued guru came up with his revelation about the New Light and the House of David.

Breault objected when the Living Prophet revealed plans to bring a thirteen-year-old Australian girl and her family to Texas to live in the compound. Aisha Gyarfas wasn't even raised as a Branch Davidian, and Breault told his guru it was unfair to bring such a young girl to the United States merely in order to have another attractive sex partner.

Surprisingly, Koresh backed down after the confrontation and told Breault he wouldn't take the girl to bed. Soon after the family moved into Mount Carmel, however, the former divinity student began to suspect the Living Prophet had lied to him.

Late one night Breault stationed himself in an office under Koresh's upstairs bedroom, and began fiddling with a computer. He wrote a couple of letters and played computer games, but his real motive for being there was to find out for himself if Koresh was cheating. Early the next morning, before daylight, Aisha walked downstairs from the Living Prophet's bedroom. Three years later, when she was sixteen, Aisha gave birth to a girl. The baby was named Startle.

By the time Koresh made his shocking announcement in La Verne that he was laying claim to married women as well as the unmarried, Breault's bride of three months was already back in her native Australia. She didn't plan to become part of the Living Prophet's harem, or to give up her husband, and she began working to earn enough money to help pay for his airfare to Australia.

Breault applied for a visa and a passport, and when they were issued a few months later he left the cult behind him for good. He packed a suitcase and a relative drove to the house in Pomona to pick him up while most of the other men who lived there were gone. Everything else, including his expensive computer, was left behind. Breault was twenty-seven years old and he had just blown away four years of his life and practically everything he owned on a fraud.

Even then, despite his disgust at the cult leader's ruthless manipulation of the Branch Davidians, Breault was nagged by self-doubts. If Koresh really was the Living Prophet or the Messiah, then Breault and his wife could be left behind when the faithful 144,000 were selected to share in the heavenly kingdom. All the suffering and sacrifice they had already undergone would be wasted.

The feeling of loss and uncertainty was typical of breakaway cultists. It takes a while to return to a normal life, even for people helped by professionals. Some families did hire experienced cult deprogrammers to help Branch Davidians leave and to assist during the transition to their new lives on the outside.

Breault and Baranyai made their decision by themselves, and they survived the difficult weaning period, but it wasn't easy. Elizabeth Baranyai later recalled that when she first rejected the cult, she was depressed and blamed God for getting her into such a mess. Gradually, her anger at God dissipated and she became thankful that he had made it possible for her to get out.

After settling down with his wife in Australia, Breault once more began attending the local Seventh-Day Adventist church and opened his own computer programming company. But neither of the cult defectors forgot the friends left behind in Texas and California. They continued to do whatever they could to help them. Breault used his computers to network with others who had left Koresh. And both husband and wife eventually began working to convince others that they could leave the destructive cult, then helped to deprogram the new refugees.

They weren't alone in their efforts. In Melbourne, Australia's oceanside city just across Bass Strait from Tasmania, Bruce and Lisa Gent had also returned home. Like Breault, when they left the United States they were disillusioned but also filled with self-doubts. Several other Australians had also kicked over the traces and were having serious second thoughts about the Living Prophet's claims to be the new Christ. The Gents and the others were also concerned about stories they had been hearing that the Branch Davidian leader was claiming all the women, single and married, for his own.

Early in 1990, the Living Prophet caught a flight to Australia and moved into the Gents' house. He had flown to Australia before to evangelize and seek recruits. This time he was on another mission. He was determined to get his uncertain disciples back. The Bible studies and marathon preaching began all over again. And Koresh confirmed the stories about the New Light, that only he should provide the seed to raise the new generation of God's children.

Lisa Gent had heard enough. She left her own home and checked into a hotel with her Bible. When she had satisfied herself through her independent reading of the Scriptures that Koresh was a false prophet, she telephoned her husband. David Koresh wasn't the Lamb, she told her mate. The Gents told Koresh he was no longer welcome in their house.

James and Michelle Tom became his new

hosts. Michelle is Lisa Gent's daughter by an earlier marriage, and she and her husband had also lived at the Texas compound with their baby. But Koresh had barely unpacked before he contacted Breault and demanded a face-to-face meeting so he could prove he was the Lamb. Breault had replaced George Roden as Koresh's new nemesis, although unlike the brooding madman in Texas, the computer expert never claimed to be a Living Prophet.

Breault and his wife, Elizabeth Baranyai, responded to the summons. When they left hours later, neither they nor Koresh had budged from their position.

A few days later Koresh flew back to the United States by himself. The trip had been a disaster. The Gents, who were wavering and unsure before he had moved in once more as their houseguest, wound up completely rejecting him even though their twin son and daughter still lived at Mount Carmel. And Breault was, if possible, even more determined to convince the remaining faithful that Howell was a hoax.

The computer programmer was especially concerned about the children, in particular the girls who were likely to be designated as brides or future brides of the polygamous leader. Kiri Jewell was one of those he was most worried about. Before defecting from the cult, he had been walking at the compound one day with the ten-year-old girl and her mother, Sherri L. Jewell, when they happened to meet Koresh. The guru asked Kiri if she was being a good girl, and she responded that she was. Koresh was pleased. She had to be a good girl if she wanted to be part of the House of David, he told her.

Koresh had begun following an ancient biblical practice called "abishag," according to the former divinity student. During King David's later years, he warmed himself on chill nights by taking young virgins to bed with him. Mahatma Gandhi, the Hindu social reformer and Indian nationalist, reportedly followed similar practices in his later years. He claimed it was a test of his vow of celibacy.

Koresh didn't share Gandhi's self-discipline. He used abishag not only as a means of keeping warm, but also as a method of preparing young virgins for their eventual initiation into the House of David, his former disciple said.

Late in 1991, Breault telephoned David S. Jewell in Niles, Michigan, and asked him if his daughter was wearing a Star of David. Jewell, a disc jockey in South Bend, Indiana, just across the state line from Niles, replied that she was.

The six-pointed Star of David, which is often formed of interlaced equilateral triangles, is known throughout the world as the symbol of

Judaism and it appears on the flag of Israel. The Living Prophet, however, used it as his personal brand of ownership for females who were already members of the House of David or were slated to become one.

To many people the star also has important mystical symbolism. Significantly, during the Middle Ages it was known as the Seal of Solomon.

David Jewell was horrified when Breault explained the significance of the symbol. She had begun wearing the Star of David when she was nine or ten years old, indicating she was slated to become a bride. She was given several, in fact, to replace some she had lost.

In 1991, Kiri was on a year-end holiday visit with her father and his new wife, Heather, when he filed suit to gain emergency custody. The radio personality had been divorced from Kiri's mother since 1982, before Sherri Jewell moved into the Branch Davidian compound with her daughter. Sherri had joined the Seventh-Day Adventist Church when she was a college student in Riverside, California, and had continued after moving to Michigan and accepting her first teaching job.

She was an intelligent, dedicated instructor who loved teaching computer and business courses. She was also serious about physical fitness and ran in triathlons.

After the divorce she took Kiri to Hawaii, where she had spent her own childhood. It was there, in the islands, where she was first exposed to Koresh's messianic evangelizing. By the time her ex-husband visited her and their daughter in the islands, Sherri was full of enthusiasm for the new religious family she had found.

During a later appearance on *Donahue* with Kiri, his sister Lois Jewell, Breault, and others, David Jewell said one of his ex-wife's favorite ways of describing her new friends had been to say they were "on fire for God." The disk jockey had attended church with his ex-wife one weekend but didn't observe anything about the new group that he considered special. Kiri was five or six years old when she and her mother moved in with the Branch Davidians in Texas.

During Kiri's regular visits in Michigan, her father was aware that she knew much more about the Scriptures than most children her age. She also had been taught that if she wore blue jeans or any other kind of long pants or shorts, she had to put on a long shirt to make sure her buttocks were modestly covered.

Kiri's aunt was concerned by the disturbing change she would observe in her niece's behavior when the girl prepared to return to Texas after her visits. "When she was packing to get back on the plane to go home, or to her mother, she would change back into this religious sort of fanatical personality," Lois Jewell told the television audience. "And it was, it was scary to watch."

Growing up in the commune, Kiri played normal childhood games, attended school and Bible study. But there were more bizarre lessons for Branch Davidian children that were chillingly reminiscent of Jim Jones and the tragedy in Guyana. Kiri recalled during her television appearance how she and other boys and girls were taught that it might someday be necessary for them to commit suicide.

Koresh directed that if a gun was used, the barrel should be stuck in her mouth, she explained. If it was held to the side of the head, there was too much chance of survival. There was also discussion of using cyanide, the girl added.

Like everyone else in the commune, she was summoned on occasion to hear the Living Prophet play his guitar. He usually stood at the center of a stage in an auditorium-like building his followers had constructed, where he played his own compositions.

Kiri was given her own fourteen-hundred-dollar guitar to practice on so that someday she could play in the cult's band. And since her father was a disk jockey, she grew up knowing how to make her own judgments about whether the music she heard was good or bad. She didn't like the shrill, ear-splitting electronic screeches produced by the Living Prophet. Kiri couldn't make out any discernible beat. Nevertheless, like everyone else she listened until he finally tired of playing. Sometimes it was the wee hours of the morning before he finally put his ax away, directed one of his lickspittle Mighty Men to summon the female he had selected for the night, and stumbled off to bed. The rest of the weary men and women would flop into their own cramped beds, often for no more than three or four hours' rest before it was time to get up again.

Being called to sit through one of the Living Prophet's impromptu command performances wasn't the worst thing about life in the commune, however. He beat children—not only Cyrus, but the children of any of his followers. Kiri was spanked hard with a wooden paddle at least once by the stern cult leader because he wasn't satisfied that she had properly memorized a Bible verse or chapter. The girl was stubborn, toughed it out, and tried not to cry.

Former disciples have claimed the cult guru once preached that it was permissible to begin beating children when they were eight months old. He sometimes used a heavy wooden spoon to whack the children. He had a space in the basement set aside for punishment, where he sometimes took children to be beaten. Cultists called it his spanking room. At other times he didn't bother taking them downstairs. He simply administered the beating wherever they happened to be at the moment.

Michelle Tom, whose home he had stayed in briefly in Melbourne, submitted an affidavit about one of the beatings; it was accepted as evidence at Kiri's custody trial in February 1992. Ironically, the trial was held in St. Joseph, Michigan, about a twenty-minute drive from Benton Harbor, where nearly a century earlier another cult leader with runaway hormones had established a House of David and sexually preyed on his female disciples.

The Toms' little girl, Tarah, was punished for thirty minutes because she cried when she had to sit on the Living Prophet's lap. According to the affidavit, the child was eight months old, and Howell beat her bottom until it bled. The young mother later said the cult leader had stopped beating the screaming infant for a moment or two every once in a while, explaining that he had to give her an opportunity to catch her breath.

Sometimes he would wind up a nasty beating

by taking the child in his arms and giving him or her a big hug. It was an example of the system of punishment and reward he had evolved for children and adults. Pimps often use the same techniques to keep their women in line and dependent on them. After a while the victims begin to believe that they deserved the punishment and will revel in the demonstration of affection as proof that despite their weakness, their abuser loves them anyway.

Breault testified about a form of abuse Howell administered to Cyrus because the three-year-old boy had refused to call Nicole Gent "Mommy" and wouldn't sit by her while she was baby-sitting. Breault said the boy's father ordered that he sleep on the kitchen floor and be left without anything to eat. After two days of the treatment, the little boy's father finally ordered Nicole to feed him. He was too weak to eat by himself.

Breault, his wife, and seventy-two-year-old Jean Smith, another former cult member from Australia, flew to the United States for the trial. Koresh's right-hand man, Steven Schneider, accompanied Sherri Jewell when she traveled to Michigan from the house in La Verne.

In his direct testimony and in an affidavit filed in support of David Jewell, Breault also described how the cult leader dissolved marriages, maintained a harem, and inflicted sexual and other physical abuse on children. He told how Koresh's male followers became virtual eunuchs, fit only to guard the master's bed.

Before the Berrien County Court trial ended, a joint custody pact was worked out to permit David and Sherri Jewell to share Kiri's custody. Judge Ronald Taylor stipulated, however, that during visits with her mother, Kiri was to be kept away from the cult leader. The girl chose to live with her father and stepmother.

Kiri was eleven years old by that time and had spent more than half her life being indoctrinated with twisted interpretations of the Scriptures and with dire warnings against backsliders and devils who rejected the Holy Word. She avoided Breault and his wife at the hearing, and it was months, after the couple made a second trip to Michigan, before she openly warmed to them.

A petite, intense woman with long dark hair, Sherri Jewell knew that her daughter had been selected as a future member of the Living Prophet's harem, Kiri eventually told the *Donahue* audience. And according to Kiri, her mother believed Koresh was Christ. Cult members usually addressed Koresh as David when they talked to him, but they considered him to be Christ, the girl said. According to breakaway members of the cult, Kiri's mother was part of Koresh's inner circle, one of his most trusted disciples.

While helping his daughter to build a new life outside the cult, David Jewell shared Breault's concern for the children left behind. When Kiri told him about two thirteen-year-old friends also targeted to become brides in the House of David, he telephoned the Texas Department of Human Services. He passed on the names of the girls and explained why he was concerned.

Government agencies received similar complaints from other former cult members. Welfare workers with the Children's Protective Services visited Mount Carmel twice to talk with the children and inspect the living arrangements. They reportedly were unable to find any evidence of abuse. Sometimes, however, authorities were more aggressive when to protecting the children caught up in the cult.

After spending the best part of her teenage years catering to the demands of the Living Prophet, giving birth to his child, and witnessing her mother moving into his harem, Robyn Bunds no longer believed Koresh's promise that one of his wives would someday be selected to become the most special woman in all humankind—the bride of Christ. Robyn Bunds wanted out!

She was living in the house in La Verne when she told Koresh about her decision to leave. She was twenty-one years old and had an outside job as a receptionist, but he scoffed at the idea that she could live on her own. In response, she tossed a name back at Koresh and said it was an old boyfriend she was going to move in with. It was untrue, but the cult leader was outraged and stalked away.

When she returned home the next day after work, her clothes and everything she owned had been removed from the house. But Koresh had played a cruel hole card. Robyn's son, Wisdom, was also gone. Children made excellent hostages for keeping mothers in line and binding them to the cult, but sometimes the women left anyway. When Kathy Jones moved to Waco and obtained a divorce, she not only left her former husband and her father behind, but her three children as well.

Robyn wasn't ready to give Wisdom up to his father. She went to the La Verne police. She reported the toddler missing, and she told them about the harem Koresh kept at the pretty house with the picket fence around it. Some of the females in the harem were under the legal age of consent, she indicated. In fact, as many as eighteen women sometimes lived at the house, and they ranged from twelve-year-old girls to women in their seventies.

Police officers accompanied her to the house,

where she pointed out the women she claimed were brides of the polygamist leader. One of them was her mother.

Koresh was upset by the appearance of the police and admitted he had sent Wisdom to Mount Carmel with Novelette Sinclair, another Branch Davidian. When he asked to speak with Robyn, the officers refused. She was being deprogrammed, they advised. They also gave the shaken cult leader forty-eight hours to get Wisdom back to California. Otherwise they would see to it that he was charged with kidnapping, and the press would be informed about the goings-on, they threatened. Wisdom was returned to his mother before the deadline.

A few days after the confrontation with Koresh, La Verne police officers returned to remove Aisha Gyarfas from the house on White Avenue. It was too late. She had already returned to Texas with the Living Prophet. But Robyn had talked with officers from the small-town police department about more than her missing son, child abuse, and harems. She had told investigators that the cult leader was violating federal laws by setting up bogus marriages with foreign nationals who wanted to come to the United States and live with the Branch Davidians. In fact, she said she had gone through a sham marriage with an Englishman in 1989, after the cult leader told her to. La Verne police passed on the information to the Immigration and Naturalization Service in Los Angeles. INS authorities later claimed they began an investigation into the allegations, but dropped it after the cult leader left the southern California area.

Less than a year after Robyn bolted the Branch Davidians, Jeannine Bunds also left. Koresh had been pestering her to bring Robyn back into the fold because it was the only way her daughter could be saved. Koresh's pressure wound up chasing Jeannine away as well. Donald Bunds, however, remained loyal to Koresh and stayed behind. A few months after Jeannine Bunds left, the cultists cleared out of the house in Pomona. Jeannine, Robyn, and Shaun moved in.

Jeannine Bunds's stepson, Robyn's half brother, Marc Bunds, had never bought Koresh's glib sales job, and he blamed the Living Prophet for stealing his father away. In 1976, when he was sixteen, he moved into Mount Carmel for a while so he could be with his father. The Rodens were in charge then and the Branch Davidians were peaceful and friendly, but after six months he left and joined the service.

Almost fifteen years had passed before he began considering a move back to Mount Carmel. He was an out-of-work electrician in Mississippi;

his motivation was a job, not religion. But after talking to his stepmother and half sister, who had already left the cult, he telephoned his father's house in California where Koresh was staying and confronted the cult leader. It was an angry exchange.

Nevertheless, Marc Bunds drove to the compound in an effort to talk to his father and see for himself what was going on. He was met at the gate by an old woman with a gun. She was on guard duty and permitted him to pass. The young electrician saw lots of guns while he was at Mount Carmel. Three days after he elbowed his way into the compound, the cultists kicked him out.

Koresh had suffered some devastating reverses, but the defectors were convinced he was a dangerous, destructive man and they were determined to break his power and rescue other former friends they had left behind. Several of the Australians banded together and in 1990 they hired a private detective.

Geoffrey Hossack began snooping around McLennan County, going through old newspaper clippings, inspecting court files, and talking with people about the Branch Davidians. In September 1990 the Australian gumshoe met with police and prosecutors at the federal courthouse in

Waco to turn over the information he had gathered during the probe. The assistant U.S. attorney, McLennan County district attorney and his chief assistant, a Department of Public Safety investigator, and a high-ranking officer with the McLennan County Sheriff's Department were present.

Hossack was armed with an impressive accumulation of information, including a thick sheaf of affidavits from former cult members accusing Koresh of viciously beating children, of having sexual relations with underage girls, and of assembling a deadly arsenal of weapons at Mount Carmel.

If the accusations were correct, there were four or five laws on the books in the state of Texas under which Koresh or others at the compound might be charged. The most severe penalties were for the aggravated sexual assault of a child, a first-degree felony. According to the statute, anyone found guilty of having sexual intercourse with a child younger than fourteen would be subject to a sentence of from five to ninety-nine years in prison. Another statute provided for a misdemeanor sentence of up to a year in the county jail for anyone with custody of a child younger than fifteen years old who places that child in danger of bodily injury or mental impairment.

Ralph Strother, the DA's right-hand man, didn't like what he was hearing at the meeting. It sounded to him as if McLennan County had its own cult, a group of religious zealots disturbingly like the Jonestown suicides. But nothing happened after the meeting. None of the assembled law enforcement officers took firm action to follow up on the accusations, explaining that the evidence that Hossack presented was not sufficient to pursue a full-scale investigation. Disappointed, but refusing to give up, Hossack resumed his investigation.

Some of the defectors began to hear talk of a list being put together of people believed to be Judases and backsliders, people who were to be punished if anything bad happened to Koresh. Breault was certain his name was at the top of the list, and he was admittedly uneasy.

But time was running out for the man the *Waco Tribune-Herald* was to label the "Sinful Messiah." His detractors, the unbelievers he referred to as "Judases" or "Babylonians," were keeping the pressure on.

Ranchers and farmers living near the compound had begun to telephone the McLennan County Sheriff's Department with reports of gunfire and explosions coming from the commune's spread. Some of the neighbors were military veterans who had served in Vietnam, and they told the law officers that the shooting was being done with M-16s and .50-caliber automatic weapons. A few days before Thanksgiving in 1992 a sheriff's deputy was driving by the area when he heard and saw an explosion set off on the property.

Inside Ranch Apocalypse, according to a close observer of the cult, Koresh had advised the faithful that Armageddon wasn't going to begin in the Holy Land as he had previously believed. It was going to begin right there on the black dirt scrubland in central Texas when they were attacked by the U.S. Army. Koresh contacted his followers in England and Australia and summoned them to Ranch Apocalypse.

Early in 1992 David Jewell wrote a letter to his local congressman, Fred Upton. Warning that a tragedy appeared to be shaping up among the Branch Davidians, he asked Upton for help convincing his congressional colleagues in Texas and California to become involved in a full-fledged investigation. The DJ explained that he had previously contacted the FBI about his fears and had received no information indicating that any action was taken.

Jewell said he was afraid the cultists were preparing for a mass suicide during their annual observance of Passover. Schneider had told family members who did not belong to the cult that they might never talk with him again because he expected his life to end soon. A young woman had also recently fled from the cultists and taken her children with her because she was afraid of a slaughter, Jewell disclosed.

Jewell also urged government authorities to look into the mistreatment of children Koresh was allegedly involved in. He attached a copy of the affidavit that Breault had submitted to the court during Kiri's custody hearing, outlining the accusations.

Upton passed the documents on to a fellow congressman from Waco, Chet Edwards. Representative Edwards sent the material to the FBI in mid-April. Edwards waited for a response until early the following February, when he sent another copy of the letter and affidavit to a different branch office of the bureau.

Again there was no response from the FBI. But a few weeks before Edwards forwarded the second set of documents to the bureau, Jewell was contacted by agents of another arm of the federal law enforcement apparatus. The ATF was interested in his story. Breault had also been contacted in Australia by the federal agency. By that time the newspaper in Waco had been conducting its own investigation of David Koresh for several months, and had developed some startling information and accusations of polygamy, pedophilia, and other abuse of children.

About the middle of February, Jewell and his daughter flew to Texas at the federal agency's expense to talk with agents. The ATF was gathering information for search and arrest warrants for the heavily armed cultists at Ranch Apocalypse. And finally, at about that time a new McLennan County district attorney had also begun a quiet investigation into the accusations of child abuse among the Branch Davidians.

Ten days after the Michigan father and his daughter flew to Texas, a small army of ATF agents drove to the isolated ranch in a convoy of cars and cattle trucks to serve their warrants.

# CHAPTER SEVEN

# The ATF

THE MEMBERS OF THE BUREAU OF ALCO-
hol, Tobacco, and Firearms, the ATF, are considered the rowdiest boys—and girls—of all the U.S.
government's highly vaunted law enforcement
officers.

The bureau provides the shock troops, the
daredevil SWAT teams that kick down doors and
burst into buildings where drug-dealing gang-
sters, terrorists, paranoid survivalists—and gun-
crazed religious fanatics—are holed up with

arsenals of high-powered automatic weapons and explosives. Or so it seems!

Of course, they're not rowdy at all. They're not even daredevils, although it might occasionally appear that way to some outsiders. They're well-trained, educated professionals picked for their courage, intelligence, and dedication to law enforcement and their country.

It's a valued old tradition!

There was a time when the professional ancestors of the ATF were called revenuers, prohibition agents, and Treasury men, or more simply, T-men.

After women's temperance activists and clergymen sold the nation on prohibition while thousands of young American males were away fighting World War I in Europe, production and trafficking in bootleg booze became one of the biggest businesses in the country.

The federal Bureau of Prohibition was charged with much of the responsibility for putting the brakes on moonshining. Agents were sent into the mountains of Appalachia and into the piney woods of Georgia and Alabama to ferret out moonshiners who produced white lightning in homemade stills and transported it in rattletrap cars souped up to outrun the revenuers.

Other T-men swooped down on smugglers

along the nation's coastlines, and on the Great Lakes where booze was being sneaked into the country from Canada.

But the most famous of all revenuers was Eliot Ness and his bribery-resistant band of agents who busted up stills, confiscated truckloads of booze, and shut down mob-supplied speakeasies in Chicago. Ness's raiders bulldozed their way into barricaded whiskey warehouses with heavy trucks used as battering rams; chopped down the locked doors of speakeasies with axes; and shot it out with bootleggers with pistols and tommy guns.

The government agents Ness led against Al Capone and other Chicago mobsters became known as the Untouchables because of their incorruptibility in a city that lived on bribes. When Ness finally put his archenemy behind bars, the end for Al Capone was undramatic. The T-man got him for cheating on his taxes.

Decades later the exploits of Ness and his straightshooters were fictionalized in a television series called *The Untouchables*. Robert Stack starred as the leader of the Chicago T-men. Today, a half-century or more after Ness's fabled battles against Chicago bootleggers, his photo still hangs in the ATF offices in Washington.

The roots of the ATF actually extend more than two hundred years back in American history, long before the time of Eliot Ness. It started after U.S. Treasury Secretary Alexander Hamilton announced a federal tax on booze in 1791. That set off the Whiskey Rebellion in western Pennsylvania led by disgruntled farmers three years later. Fifteen thousand militiamen were called up to put the insurrection down and save the unpopular tax.

In 1802, during President Thomas Jefferson's first term of office, the tax was dropped. Beer and stronger "spirits" then remained levy free in the United States for approximately sixty years until the tax was reinstated to help finance the Civil War. The federal government then hired three detectives to track down liquor tax cheats.

That was almost a half-century before the Office of the Chief Examiner, the predecessor of the FBI, was established in July 1908.

For the next eight decades, ferreting out moonshiners and other liquor tax evaders, along with enforcing various other trade, labeling, and advertising laws, continued to be the lone mission of the federal liquor taxing enforcement agency that developed from its modest three-man beginnings.

There were occasional name changes, however. And after the production and sale of alcoholic beverages was again legalized in most states in 1933, the Bureau of Prohibition that the

Untouchables had made so famous was renamed the Alcohol Tax Unit.

The biggest and most critical change in the agency's mission, one that would eventually lead to the showdown outside Ranch Apocalypse, occurred in 1942 during the early years of World War II. That was when the bureau was charged with enforcing federal laws regulating the ownership, sale, purchase, and use of firearms.

As employees of the federal bureau responsible for enforcing gun laws, the agents also began conducting investigations into smuggling and manufacture of illegal narcotics. The agency continued to play a major role in the suppression of drug trafficking, until a new arm of the federal law enforcement apparatus that would eventually become the Drug Enforcement Agency was formed.

In the meantime, the agency that produced Eliot Ness and the Untouchables was continuing to undergo change. In 1951 it was given responsibility for overseeing and enforcing the federal regulations governing production and taxation of tobacco. A new name, the Alcohol and Tobacco Tax Division, came along with the new job responsibilities.

In 1972 it was at last given full bureau status in the U.S. Treasury Department and was renamed the Bureau of Alcohol, Tobacco, and Firearms. At that time the U.S. Treasury Department also took over much of the enforcement responsibilities of the Internal Revenue Service. Ten years later the ATF was also given responsibility for investigation of commercial arson.

By that time the FBI had begun to lose some of the glamour that had been attached to it since the exciting days when agents gunned down John Dillinger in a Chicago alley and helped capture Bruno Hauptmann, the kidnapper of the Lindbergh baby. They were busy chasing spies, investigating blue-collar crime, and leaning on the leaders of corrupt labor unions. FBI agents almost never shot anyone with tommy guns anymore, and they were more likely to be lawyers and CPAs in business suits than daring gunslingers.

Despite its older history, the ATF somehow became the new kids on the block. When bigtime drug traffickers barricaded themselves in a slum building or warehouse with an arsenal of automatic and semiautomatic weapons, it was the ATF that joined with the DEA and local officers to shoot it out.

By the early 1990s, the U.S. Treasury Department enforcement arm boasted forty-two hundred employees, about half of them agents. ATF agents complete a course at the Federal Law Enforcement Training Center in Georgia. They are also trained with army special operations teams.

Agents work out of twenty-one field offices and five regional offices while keeping an eye on an estimated two hundred million firearms owned by Americans. By the time the shootout occurred at the cult compound, more than 286,000 people and businesses owned legal firearms licenses, and fifteen hundred new applications were being processed every month.

Thousands of other guns were in circulation illegally. But there are so many guns and sales transactions that convicted criminals and the mentally ill are often able to purchase weapons by simply lying on their applications. There aren't enough enforcement officers to keep up with the flood of sales and purchases.

Nevertheless, when President Reagan was shot in 1981, it took the ATF only twenty minutes of record checking to trace the gun to a pawnshop in Dallas where it had been sold to John W. Hinckley, Jr.

The ATF is best known among rank-and-file Americans, however, for the courageous street work of its agents. They set up dangerous law enforcement stings; work undercover infiltrating some of the more violent elements within the neo-Nazi and American Communist movements or the Ku Klux Klan; swoop down on fanatical survivalists who are heavily armed and spoiling for a fight; and go after barricaded tax protestors who vow to defend their views with guns and their lives.

During the turbulent upheavals of the late 1960s and early 1970s, they were one of the premier law enforcement agencies charged with controlling fanatical Weather Underground bombers, gun-toting Black Panthers, and other violent radical groups.

They have been kept busiest during the past few years trying to keep powerful automatic weapons out of the hands of narcotics traffickers who tend to drive by street corners and eliminate competitors by leaning out of cars and spraying everyone in sight, enemy or innocent bystander, with automatic weapons fire.

The ATF works on society's cutting edge, and its agents are often confronted by heavily armed zealots who would rather shoot than negotiate. Unavoidably, their mission and the way they must carry it out has led to bitter criticism from a disparate range of civil libertarians and other faultfinders.

In the early 1980s, U.S. Senate hearings were held to probe accusations of Rambo-style tactics by ATF agents while enforcing gun laws. A critical report was subsequently returned and some changes were made in operational methods. But it's unlikely the ATF will ever experience more vitriol and anger than the storm of criticism and Monday-morning quarterbacking that erupted after the wild shootout at Ranch Apocalypse. Along with the staggering loss of life and the numerous injuries to other agents, the ATF's image was heading for a devastating battering.

Since the high-profile days of the Bureau of Prohibition, about 120 revenuers, T-men, and their professional descendants have been killed in the line of duty. But there was never a day like Bloody Sunday, when four agents died and more than a dozen others were injured.

The country's new national leader, President Bill Clinton, quickly stepped into the picture, directing the FBI to take over command of the operation outside the barricaded compound. He issued an order to withhold taking any new action that might add to the death toll among the rapidly growing army of law enforcement officers ringing Ranch Apocalypse.

Although U.S. law pinpoints the FBI as the investigative body with responsibility for probing assaults on most federal officers, the ATF is an exception. FBI press officers, however, claimed the ATF had asked for the bureau's help. FBI Director William Sessions, a former federal judge from Texas whose own position in Washington was shaky, told the press the bureau was "sharing the responsibility" at the scene with the ATF.

FBI Special Agent Jeffrey J. Jamar, a native Texan and chief of the bureau's San Antonio office, took over the operation outside the cult compound as the field director. Lloyd Bentsen, the new treasury secretary and former longtime U.S. senator from Texas, told the press that the president was being regularly briefed on the emergency.

Although ATF spokesmen were officially mum about the abrupt change of command, some journalists and Capitol Hill observers saw the move as an embarrassing slap in the face for a bureau already locked in bitter interagency rivalries and fiercely defending the rapid burgeoning of its staff and budget in recent years. As recently as the Reagan administration there had been serious talk of abolishing the bureau and splitting up its responsibilities between the Secret Service and Customs.

The ATF survived that scare, but like other federal law enforcement agencies and the military, by early 1993 it was anticipating deep cuts in its new budget to comply with the Clinton administration's promise to reduce spending. At a time when the bureau was locked in an unprecedentedly lengthy siege that was costing nearly $400,000 a week in overtime, travel, and extra equipment, administrators were faced with the prospect of slicing a minimum of $3.8 million from annual expenditures.

At a press conference a couple of days after the shootout, Jamar outlined the government's goal as avoiding further bloodshed and ultimately settling things with the Branch Davidians in federal court. It wouldn't do any good to set a deadline for ending the siege, he said.

Dan Hartnett, associate director of the ATF, echoed Jamar's remark that the element of surprise had been lost when someone telephoned a tip to the cultists Sunday morning before the raid. "There is no doubt they were expecting our arrival," the high-ranking ATF executive told the assembled reporters. A black band of mourning was taped to Hartnett's badge as he talked.

Hartnett also pointed out another disadvantage the raiding party had to deal with after the shooting started. They had to be especially careful to pick out specific targets before shooting, because of fears that an indiscriminate rain of gunfire might injure the women and children known to be inside the buildings. The rapid-firing cultists had no such problem.

One sad example of the reluctance to shoot possible noncombatants came to light when a bureau official revealed that senior agents monitoring the operation from helicopters were watching a cultist with a rifle. They withheld permission for snipers to shoot him because he didn't appear to be behaving aggressively. Then he shot Agent Willis, and an ATF sniper was given the go-ahead to fire. The cultist was killed.

The ATF hadn't even buried its dead before high-ranking officers found themselves defending their actions and trying to explain the tragic and embarrassing performance in the confrontation with the cultists. Nor did all the sniping aimed at the ATF end with the cease-fire, or with the second brief skirmish at the compound. The verbal sniping couldn't match the cultists' sharpshooting for deadliness, but it was more widespread and it lasted longer.

People from the area who talked to reporters— nearby farmers and ranchers as well as Waco's small-business community—were nearly unanimous in describing the cultists as pleasant folks who generally kept to themselves, behaved well when they were in town, and paid their bills in cash.

Vic Feazell, a lawyer in Austin who is a former McLennan County district attorney, angrily scored the ATF operation as a "storm trooper" attack. They were merely protecting what was theirs, the onetime clergyman said of the shooting. "They're protective of their land. They view it as Muslims do Mecca and Jews view Jerusalem."

He called the raid a vulgar display of power by the federal agents, which he said the Branch Davidians met with fear and paranoia.

Retired Lieutenant Colonel Charles Beckwith, who established the army's crack Delta Force, added his voice to the growing crush of ATF critics. In nationally broadcast interviews and talks with reporters, the former Special Forces commander blamed the ATF's action-oriented style for apparently leading to the ambush, and said it would have been better if the FBI had been in charge from the beginning. "I certainly wouldn't have gone in there with guns blazing—that's crazy," the crusty Austin resident declared.

ATF spokeswoman Sharon Wheeler unintentionally added fuel to the controversy after reporters asked her at a news conference in Waco why the assault had gone so dreadfully wrong. "I don't believe we were outmanned or outplanned. The problem we had was that we were outgunned," she said. Later expanding on her remarks, she added, "Obviously, they had bigger guns than we did."

After Ms. Wheeler's remarks appeared in the press, another ATF spokesman in Washington quickly announced an amendment. Tom Hill told reporters that her comments about the weaponry should not be taken literally. And the ATF's Jack Killorin said the problem wasn't that the strike force was outgunned, but that they didn't share the willingness of the cultists for widescale bloodshed. The ATF could have won the fight if it wished to, and if it hadn't been concerned about the lives of the cultists inside the buildings, he indicated.

Several government agents who participated in the strike, however, backed up Wheeler's statement after receiving assurances they wouldn't be identified in news articles. They complained that they were sent off with pistols, sniper rifles, shotguns, and a few semiautomatics to face the awesome firepower of the barricaded cultists. Their requests for more powerful and rapid-fire weapons had been turned down.

The agents were quoted anonymously as denouncing the ATF hierarchy for faulty planning and flawed decisions right up to the last minutes before the raid. Even though supervisors knew the element of surprise was lost, they ordered the assault anyway, according to the agents. Their lives were needlessly endangered, they complained.

In *The New York Times*, several agents compared the abortive assault to the Charge of the Light Brigade, because planning and launching of the operation was so riddled with high-level blunders. In Dallas, editors with the ABC and NBC affiliate stations disclosed that they had been notified by Ms. Wheeler the day before the raid that something big was shaping up. Although she didn't tell them what, when, or exactly where, she reportedly advised them to get ready to cover a major story. In Washington, a bureau spokesman conceded that "Gonzales" had informed his superiors that the cultists were told about the planned raid ahead of time. Senior ATF officers decided to go ahead with the operation anyway, he said, because despite the apparent tip-off, the cultists seemed to be following their normal morning routine.

Although area law enforcement officers were discussing the impending foray on their radios nearly an hour before it occurred, the spokesman said no evidence was uncovered to indicate that their broadcasts had led to the cultists being alerted.

But the flak continued coming from all sides. Verbal brickbats were tossed at planners for reputedly setting up a poor communications system. Only squad leaders were supplied with walkie-talkies, and when they were put out of action the link to other teams was broken, the critics claimed. An ATF spokesman responded to the accusation by stating that each agent had a working radio that could be used to communicate with his or her colleagues.

The ATF was accused of failing to fully inform all agents about contingency plans in case they were met with heavy resistance, and not even telling some members of the assault team about the military-style weapons in the cultists' arsenal. Other critics blamed planners for failing to take along a physician or to arrange ahead of time for an aid station on the scene. The FBI typically provides for that type of medical care when it is involved in operations where shooting is anticipated.

A high-ranking ATF agent responded to those complaints by pointing out that each team involved in the assault had an emergency technician assigned to it, including one EMT who was a surgical nurse. Ambulances were also parked a few hundred yards down the road from the compound, and a medical helicopter was on call.

Even the timing of the raid was criticized, again by anonymous detractors, who said it should have been launched late at night when most of the occupants of the compound would presumably be asleep.

The *Tribune-Herald* helped stir up another fuss because the National Guard had provided helicopters, which are traditionally loaned to federal agencies only when illegal narcotics are involved. For weeks after the raid, federal authorities had told the press there was no suspicion of illegal drugs at the ranch, the newspaper reported. Then, after state authorities in Austin began talking of being misled by the ATF, the agency came up with a different story for the press. ATF spokesmen said they had suspected the presence of a methamphetamine laboratory inside the compound. An aerial infrared scan had revealed a hot spot like those created by laboratories used for producing and refining the drug, the ATF claimed.

The ATF, through its spokesmen, publicly criticized the *Waco Tribune-Herald* for not delaying publication until after the raid. ATF agents claimed that someone from the media had made the late-Sunday-morning telephone call overheard by the undercover man calling himself Gonzales, the call that tipped off the cult. And they criticized the *Waco Tribune-Herald* for refusing their plea to hold off the "Sinful Messiah" series and consequently alerting the cultists that they were liable to be raided.

Less than three weeks after the firefight, Agent Risenhoover filed a fifteen-page lawsuit accusing an unnamed *Tribune-Herald* employee or employees of warning the cultists that the raid was about to occur. The injured ATF man claimed to have proof to back up his accusation, although it was not spelled out in the court documents.

Waco attorney James R. Dunham, who filed the suit, said his client was filing the legal action because he believed his injuries might leave him with permanent damage. Although the suit asked for actual and punitive damages, no specific amount of money was specified. Risenhoover also claimed in the suit that reporters and photographers for the newspaper were near the compound an hour or more before the ATF convoy arrived and told one of the cultists or one of their sympathizers that the operation was about to be launched. In typical legalese, the suit stated:

> Said member and/or sympathizer immediately went into the compound, whereupon all children who were at that time playing on the compound grounds were immediately called inside the compound buildings.
>
> The conduct of the *Waco Tribune-Herald* warned and notified the occupants of the compound that a raid was to be conducted and enabled the occupants to prepare and forcibly resist the ATF agents and other law enforcement officials.

Risenhoover also accused the newspaper of breaking an agreement not to publish articles stemming from its own investigation of the cultists:

> The *Waco Tribune-Herald* knew and should have known of the dangerous situation which existed at the compound and the *Waco Tribune-Herald* knew and should have known that the publication of their proposed series on their investigation would alert David Koresh and the occupants of the compound and would heighten the potential for violence since said series of articles were [*sic*] very inflammatory toward both David Koresh and the Branch Davidian sect.

*Tribune-Herald* editor Bob Lott quickly denied responsibility on the part of the newspaper for tipping the government's hand to the cultists. In a prepared statement, Lott said, "The injuries to agent Risenhoover and the deaths of and injuries to others are regrettable, but they were not caused by this paper."

Lott also firmly denied that the newspaper had agreed with the agency not to publish the series. "The ATF knows that we had no such agreement. We notified the ATF the afternoon before publication," he said. According to the editor, the ATF asked the newspaper about a month before the operation to delay the series. The series was ultimately held back about a month, although the delay was for other reasons, he said. Lott didn't specify what those reasons were. In Washington, an ATF spokesman also said there was no agreement to scrub the series.

Risenhoover's suit was amended a few weeks later and named Mark England as the reporter who allegedly tipped off one of the cultists or a sympathizer that the ATF was on the way. England, who was a coauthor of the "Sinful Messiah" series, firmly denied the accusation, calling it "preposterous." England said the intent of the newspaper in conducting the lengthy investigation and printing the series was to warn the people in the community about the cult leader.

Branch Davidian member Kathryn Schroeder revealed through her lawyer that another Branch Davidian outside the compound had been driving nearby and stopped to talk with someone inside a white van or Blazer on a farm road close to the compound. It was that cult member who had telephoned the warning to Koresh, she reportedly said. The person inside the van was not identified.

Journalists around the country rallied to the support of the Waco newspaper with statements and editorials. Jane Kirtley, executive director of the Reporters Committee for the Freedom of the Press, claimed the suit and the accusations it contained challenged the press's independent role.

Questions were asked in the press, as well, about why the telephones in the compound hadn't been tapped by law enforcement agencies. The ATF responded to that by pointing out that a wiretap would have been rejected by the courts because the telephones were unlikely to turn up any information that couldn't be ferreted out by the undercover agents. The nation's courts jealously guard the privacy of citizens and don't indiscriminately approve orders to tap telephones.

In Washington, D.C., the ATF moved to distance itself from the lawsuit. Ms. Wheeler told reporters the suit was "strictly between the agent and the newspaper." She refused to answer a question about whether or not Risenhoover had sought permission from his employer to file the action. But ATF Intelligence Chief David Troy didn't mince words defending the bureau's decision to move on the heavily fortified compound and in blaming someone in the media for tipping its hand.

"The critics might say, why didn't we just send a registered letter . . . 'Dear [David], you've been a bad boy, why don't you come on out?' " he scoffed.

Moving on to the devastating failure to catch the cultists napping, he added: "We would have had control of that compound within sixty seconds or less had there not been a prior tip-off to the compound that there was an impending raid. We feel confident there were no mistakes made on our part."

Early in March, high-ranking bureau officers told a similar story to a congressional subcommittee that oversees the Treasury Department and was reviewing the AFT budget request for 1994. ATF Director Stephen E. Higgins, a veteran lawman who has headed the bureau since 1982 and has three presidential citations, warned the lawmakers that more slaughter was inevitable unless the flood of firearms and explosives was kept out of the hands of criminals and fanatics.

"The guns of Waco and the bombs of New York are too readily available," he cautioned. "We must deal with these criminals or they will deal with us." The reference to New York was sparked by the bombing of the World Trade Center in Manhattan that killed six people and injured more than a thousand on February 26, only two days before the bloodbath at Ranch Apocalypse.

In a subsequent appearance before a U.S. Senate appropriations subcommittee, Higgins repeated much the same story as he defended the bureau against the storm of accusations. When

Arizona Democrat and panel chairman Dennis DeConcini asked why the commando team didn't call on the Texas National Guard for help, and why it wasn't better armed to counter the cultists' powerful weapons, Higgins cited fears of injuring the women and children.

"It's important for people to understand there's a big difference between assaulting this place with intent to eliminate these people versus going in and trying to make an arrest," he declared.

"We wanted to protect lives, not to take them," said the thirty-one-year agency veteran.

By that time, *Newsweek* magazine had reported that some members of the assault team might have been hit by so-called friendly fire. Higgins strongly denied there was any evidence to back up the reports. He told the panel the ATF had carried out more than two hundred major raids prior to the shootout near Waco, and suffered only one injury.

Other bureau spokesmen, including Troy, echoed the denials about friendly fire casualties in interviews with the press. The outspoken intelligence chief didn't pull any punches. The only thing more ridiculous he could think of than the friendly fire report, he scoffed, was that Koresh "thinks he is the Lamb of God, when all he is is a cheap thug who interprets the Bible through the barrel of a gun."

On Capitol Hill, Higgins refused to reply to some questions from the senators dealing with specifics of the raid. He didn't want to jeopardize the investigations that were going on, he explained. The Texas Rangers were probing the debacle. The Rangers were also the agency with responsibility for the homicide investigation stemming from the gun battle, and they were probing the alleged leak to the cultists about the impending raid.

Secretary Bentsen furthermore pledged that after the siege was broken, the Treasury Department would see to it that a thorough and independent review was undertaken of the entire affair, from planning and strategy to the flawed execution of the raid.

The ATF chief insisted to the panel that there was no cover-up. DeConcini and his Republican colleague, Senator Christopher Bond of Missouri, made statements at the hearing defending Higgins against the firestorm of anonymous accusations being bandied about in the press.

In Texas, some critics were claiming there was no reason for the raid in the first place. Koresh made frequent trips to Elk or Waco to shop or relax, attended gun shows, and often jogged outside the compound, they said. If the ATF wanted him, agents could have swooped down on him outside Ranch Apocalypse and almost surely arrested him without a struggle. An area clergyman told reporters it was commonly known that Koresh jogged and engaged in other activities outside. He said he thought the government had deliberately set out to demonstrate a show of force.

Initially, ATF spokesmen said Koresh had holed up in the compound for months, so there was no opportunity to pick him up outside. But too many of Koresh's neighbors had seen him away from Ranch Apocalypse, as did shopkeepers and restaurateurs who did business with him. The ATF admitted they hadn't conducted full-time surveillance of the cult leader in advance of the encounter.

Other ATF detractors pointed to the earlier shootout between the rival factions at the compound, when Sheriff Harwell used the telephone to talk Koresh into peacefully surrendering and giving up his arms.

Although the warrants used as the basis for the assault were sealed by court order, the ATF chief talked on CBS television's long-running show *48 Hours* about the motivation for the raid. The Branch Davidians could have stored scores or hundreds of weapons without breaking federal firearm laws, he said. It was their conversion of semiautomatic firearms to automatic that got them into trouble with the law.

The ATF leader's remarks on the television show and other statements and documents alleged that Shooters Equipment in Westminster, South Carolina, had sold parts to the cultists that could be used to convert semiautomatic weapons to full automatic. The alteration permits the uninterrupted firing of a string of bullets from a cartridge clip by simply depressing and holding the trigger. On semiautomatic, the trigger must be pressed to fire, then released, and pressed again to fire another bullet.

And enough parts to convert fifty AR-15s into short-barreled rifles similar to those used by police SWAT teams were sold by an Olympia, Washington, company to an auto shop called the Mag Bag, operated by Woodrow Kendrick, a few miles from the compound. AR-15s are virtually the same as the military's M-16 .223-caliber assault rifles.

Kendrick and some other men lived at the Mag Bag. Howell and other cultists reportedly sometimes tinkered up the engines of their cars, motorcycles, and other vehicles there. Government authorities, however, suspected it held another arms cache. A few days after the raid they used a Bradley tank to smash their way into the building. They were serving a search warrant, and this time they were careful not to take any unnecessary risks. They didn't find anything but a few shotgun shells.

Although Olympic Arms didn't sell any parts to the Mag Bag for conversion of weapons from semiautomatic to automatic, the ATF believed that the cultists had traded elsewhere for some aptly named "hellfire switches." The spring and screw devices cost about twenty-five to forty dollars each and can be trigger mounted to convert semiautomatic weapons for so-called simulated automatic fire. Hellfire switches, which are easily available at gun shows, are legal because they can be used without altering the internal mechanism of the weapon.

The switches trigger the gun electrically, permitting firing ten to twenty times faster than a shooter could accomplish using his or her finger with a semiautomatic weapon. The shooter's finger doesn't touch the trigger when hellfire switches are used. Many weapons aficionados, however, say hellfire switches adversely affect accuracy, and firing of an entire clip of bullets is likely to result in only a couple of hits on a target.

Hellfire switches aren't always necessary, however, because fully automatic and other high-powered weapons are available for people who have the money and know where to look. Some can be purchased legally, such as a Barrett .50-caliber rifle, which can fire shells capable of penetrating light armored vehicles. The cultists purchased a .50-caliber from a wholesaler in the Dallas area. But there is a thriving American black market in illegal weapons with equal or more devastating firepower.

Various gun dealers around the country, most speaking privately, have acknowledged that just about anything someone like Koresh might want to buy can easily be bought. Thousands of illegal AK-47s made in China are said to have been smuggled or somehow otherwise imported into the country. Other high-powered and automatic weapons have been stolen from military supplies and are available on the black market for people who can pay the price.

As the pressure on the ATF built up, some curious stories made their way into the press: the reputed methamphetamine lab; big-time drug dealing; a money-laundering operation; and a crazed scheme by the Branch Davidians to launch a bloody attack on Waco that would make the Los Angeles riots "look like child's play." No specific reason was spelled out for a planned massacre of churchgoing residents of the city some still call "Jerusalem on the Brazos." But there was some speculation that, driven by their fanatical belief in the Second Advent and the

Apocalypse, the cultists might have decided it was time to massacre the Babylonians, or unbelievers.

But critics of the ATF were coming out of the woodwork, and the bureau's increasingly desperate efforts at damage control were meeting with spotty success at best. The ATF had been dealing with criticism from various civil rights and gun rights forces for years. As the key federal law enforcement agency with responsibility to control trafficking or ownership or illegal guns, the ATF made many enemies. The United States is a nation of guns, where powerful forces are at work on both sides of the controversy over their control. There are some circles where the ATF is virtually equated with Satan.

An officer of an organization called the Second Amendment Foundation remarked in the *Houston Post* that the ATF wasn't "very subtle about certain things." Tim Sekerak, legal affairs director for the group, said the ATF was known for storming through doors and expecting the occupants to cower.

The Second Amendment to the Constitution establishes the right to bear arms and is at the core of the enmity between the ATF and many of its critics. The amendment states; "A well-regulated militia being necessary to the security of a free State, the right of the people to keep and bear arms, shall not be infringed."

The right to bear arms was also written into the Texas Constitution when the former republic became a state in 1845. As it appears today, after an amendment was written into it shortly after the end of the Civil War, it states: "Every citizen shall have the right to keep and bear arms in the lawful defense of himself or the state; but the Legislature shall have power, by law, to regulate the wearing of arms with a view to prevent crime."

Critics who in the wake of the raid, raised their voices in defense of the cultists also pointed to other liberties expressly protected under the Bill of Rights, including the First Amendment. It reads in part: "Congress shall make no law respecting an establishment of religion, or prohibiting the free exercise thereof; or abridging the freedom of speech, or of the press; or the right of the people peaceably to assemble, and to petition the government for redress of grievances."

Some complained that the government was trampling on the Branch Davidians' religious freedom, and others grumbled about the sanctity of the home and Bill of Rights protections against unreasonable search and seizure. The controversy filled the letters-to-the-editor columns of newspapers throughout Texas; and callers kept telephone lines busy on radio talk shows, clamoring to contribute their two cents worth in the debate swirling around the flawed raid on the compound.

Some writers and callers sided with the ATF officers, calling them courageous patriots defending their countrymen against crazed religious fanatics who were armed to the teeth and ready to die in a holy war, people who lived by their own warped laws. Others criticized the ATF, calling them everything from Nazi storm troopers, to baby killers and Rambo-inspired goons who were happily trampling all over the Bill of Rights.

After the ghastly debacle at Ranch Apocalypse, the ATF was wounded and vulnerable, and protesters with signs and leaflets began showing up at the Federal Building in Dallas, at government buildings in other cities, and outside the police barricades surrounding the compound near Waco. Most accused the ATF of violating constitutionally protected religious freedoms and the right to bear arms.

One man driving outside the police perimeters around the compound tossed a handful of leaflets from his car. The message on the leaflets was curt, blunt, and impossible to misinterpret. "Attention: BATF murderers! Get out of Texas and take Ann Richards with you," they said. Ann Richards is the state's Democratic governor.

Demonstrators who arrived in cars, pickup trucks, and Blazers a few days later used megaphones and carried signs blasting the ATF. ATF KILLS BABIES, said one sign. ATF IS NOT JESUS EITHER, proclaimed another. Most of the protesters were from the San Antonio area, and many wore red-and-white armbands with the words UNARMED PATRIOT.

There was more of the same in Dallas, where demonstrators shuffled back and forth in front of the federal courthouse. IS YOUR CHURCH ATF APPROVED?; IMPRISON ATF TERRORISTS, and R.I.P. THE BILL OF RIGHTS, WACO, TX 1993 were inscribed on some of the signs. The R.I.P. slogan was scrawled on a drawing of a leaning tombstone.

Some of the lunch-hour demonstrators in the state's second-largest city identified themselves as members of the Libertarian Party, the North Texas Arms Rights Coalition, the Associated Conservatives of Texas, and various other groups, or merely as private citizens. They were united, however, in their distaste for the ATF and the assault on Ranch Apocalypse. Libertarians also picketed at the Waco Convention Center, carrying American flags and signs calling for the ATF to be disbanded. The marchers proclaimed, "Please: No more macho cops."

Demonstrators also showed up near Texas Department of Public Safety checkpoints a couple of miles from the compound with signs supporting the ATF, but they were outnumbered. Once after eight or nine men and women near the barricades began waving slogans thanking the ATF for the courage of its agents, about twenty people led by a fundamentalist preacher from Fort Worth showed up to demonstrate against the agency. The Reverend W. N. Otwell emerged soon after the shootout as one of the leading and most outspoken critics of the agency. He took on the media as well, accusing reporters and editors of settling for spoon-fed information from the government.

Critics of the agency were more visibly active than its defenders. And they were among the vanguard of a curiously eclectic horde that began descending on Waco and the besieged fortress within a few hours of the deadly encounter.

# CHAPTER EIGHT

# The Siege

*There is not going to be a violent end, at least as far as David is concerned. There's not going to be anybody hurt.*

—Dick DeGuerin
David Koresh's lawyer

AS THE FBI TOOK OVER CONTROL OF OPerations outside the Branch Davidian compound, the government continued building its forces and digging in for a prolonged siege.

Additional M2AO Bradley infantry fighting vehicles with tracks were brought in from Fort Hood by the Texas National Guard to replace lighter-armored M113 personnel carriers. M2A0s are constructed to withstand .50-caliber armorpiercing bullets; the personnel carriers are not. Federal agents were given rapid courses in operation of the vehicles, which normally carry crews of three. The guard also provided UH-1 Bell helicopters to the ATF.

The FBI quickly squelched rumors that the heavier tanklike vehicles would be used to shoot and smash an entryway into the compound. Spokesmen pointed out that mounted machine guns and automatic cannons had been removed and the vehicles weren't equipped with the normal load of antitank missiles. They were borrowed for defensive purposes only, it was explained.

Portable toilets, sandbags, gasoline, and other equipment and supplies were hauled into the area by truck. A couple of recreational vehicles pulled up a little later. Then a bulldozer was brought in.

Texas Rangers, McLennan County Sheriff's Department deputies, and U.S. marshals also joined the rapidly burgeoning interagency effort to extract the barricaded cultists. The Waco Police Department continued to provide additional support in the city.

The federal agencies continued to use the Texas State Technical Institute as their main operations area and set up regular press conferences at the Waco Convention Center. Some students and faculty joked that with all the police officers around, Texas State Tech boasted the safest campus in the world.

During the early days of the standoff, authorities estimated it was costing the ATF and the FBI about a half-million dollars each per week. And the per-week costs were expected to climb the longer the crisis continued. The Greater Waco Chamber of Commerce estimated that the combined total, one million dollars, was the approximate amount of money being added to the local economy each week by the influx of people attracted to the city by the crisis at Ranch Apocalypse.

At the state psychiatric hospital at Vernon, George Roden starred in an "I told you so" press conference. "They didn't believe me then. I think they do now," Roden gloated. During an hour long meeting with reporters he accused Koresh of using classic methods of brainwashing including sleep deprivation, of intimidating his followers, and of setting different rules for them and for himself.

"He converted the leadership to Nazism," Roden declared. "That's why I find myself in here at this time."

As guards and a doctor watched closely, Roden claimed he still had enough support from Branch Davidians to resume leadership. "He's no Jesus Christ. He never has been, he never will be," the deposed cult leader declared about Koresh. "He's not Jesus Christ any more than Satan is."

Nearer to Ranch Apocalypse, authorities continued to restrict the growing number of reporters to the outside of barricades set up along farm roads nearly two miles from the scene of the shoot-out. Eventually reporters established their own disorganized settlement of cars, vans, and lawn chairs that was unofficially dubbed Satellite City. Joe Duncan, a hirsute free-lance television photographer from Houston who was on the job for NBC-TV, assumed the title of mayor and took up a collection to raise money for garbage disposal.

The reporters, who arrived from the United Kingdom, Canada, and Australia as well as from throughout the United States, were in the vanguard of a ragtag and bobtail collection of modern-day camp followers, dilettantes, entrepreneurs, and would-be peacemakers who were attracted to the standoff site like bees to honey.

A few yards outside the barricades and in Waco, members of the press, families of injured law officers and holed-up cultists, along with the horde of ATF and FBI agents were given a pleasant taste of Texas hospitality. The people of Waco, suburban Bellmead, and other nearby communities didn't ask for the shoot-out and siege to occur, but they responded to the crisis with magnanimity and sympathy.

Community prayer services for the safety of the cultists were held, and clergymen banded together to raise funds for the families of the slain ATF men. Hillcrest Baptist Medical Center provided rooms at the Magnolia Inn on the hospital grounds for relatives of injured ATF agents. When those rooms ran out, the relatives, as well as some journalists who couldn't find space in motels, were given private rooms in the maternity ward. The Waco Baptist Association rounded up clergymen to help comfort families of the dead and injured.

Coming forward in organized groups and individually, residents of the city on the Brazos took other actions to make things easier on visitors caught up in events surrounding the siege. Sammy Citrano, owner of Waco's Elite Cafe, began cooking up huge pots of Tex-Mex food, then drove it to the barricades and passed it out to hungry law enforcement officers. Other restaurants sent barbecue, pastries, coffee, soft drinks, and lasagne. The Extension Homemakers of McLennan County baked hundreds of potatoes for the men and women on the barricades.

Motels were already stretched to the limit by reservations from people planning to attend a five-day Texas–New Mexico Junior College Basketball Championship tournament beginning the first week of March. The few rooms that were left quickly filled up with agents from the ATF and FBI, Texas Rangers, other law officers, and the press. When the rooms ran out, private citizens provided shelter and beds in their own homes for out-of-town reporters. Free tickets were also distributed to reporters and photographers to attend the annual festival, "Taste of Waco."

Citizens flocked to the Red Cross to donate blood and replenish supplies used treating the injured ATF agents. Near the compound, a woman barber from Houston gave free haircuts to reporters and law officers. The Salvation Army set up shop and passed out free coffee and food. Ranch Apocalypse was out in the boondocks, where hungry law officers and reporters couldn't even buy a Twinkie. There weren't any restaurants around, and the closest general store was four or five miles away in Elk.

Seventh-Day Adventist leaders and clergy, meanwhile, were horrified at news of the slaughter and quickly moved to distance themselves from the fanatical cult leader and his followers. Other Davidians and Branch Davidians around the nation who had broken off from the leadership at Mount Carmel or had gone their own way long before, also hurried to explain to the press that they they weren't followers of Koresh. Some of the concerned Davidians who traced their spiritual genesis to Houteff, most of them native Jamaicans, lived as close to the action as Waco. Others were scattered around the country, usually in small towns or rural areas like Mountaindale, New York, and in the Ozark Mountains of Missouri, where a small community of devout believers were known as Davidian Seventh-Day Adventists.

In Keene, Southwestern Adventist College paid for a three-quarter-page newspaper ad renouncing the cultists and extending sympathy to families of the slain ATF men. "David Koresh and his followers have no connection with the Seventh-Day Adventist Church," the statement said in part.

Similar statements were made by clergy and elders of Seventh-Day Adventist schools and congregations around the country, in the United Kingdom, and in other countries. No one wanted to claim David Koresh and "God's marines" for their own.

Hollywood hotshots with their checkbooks in their hands sought out former cultists and family members, anyone they could find to help put together a quick made-for-television movie. Robyn Bunds was quoted in the press saying she was juggling a couple of offers for TV films and another from a movie producer. And Koresh complained to federal negotiators about what he claimed was exploitation after he heard reports that his mother was offered seventy-five thousand dollars for movie rights.

The first movie to get off the ground in the Hollywood scramble was a film titled *In the Line of Duty: Ambush in Waco*. NBC had already shown five earlier films in its *In the Line of Duty* series about the deaths of law enforcement officers. The three-and-a-half-week shoot for the NBC movie began in April in Mounds, Oklahoma, where the Bethesda Boys Ranch was altered to resemble Ranch Apocalypse. Timothy Daly, star of the second-season sitcom *Wings*, was cast as Koresh.

Meanwhile, in Waco and out near the barricades, jobless men, college students, and housewives set up shop from makeshift stands and the backs of pickup trucks and vans, selling sandwiches, pizza, soft drinks, T-shirts, caps, and other souvenirs of the standoff. Some of the most popular shirts and caps bore the slogan

We
Ain't
Comin'
Out.

Depending on the vendor, white T-shirts could usually be purchased for about ten or twelve dollars. Color shirts cost a couple of dollars more. Near some of the T-shirt vendors a team of enterprising men hawked Koresh burgers and Koresh dogs for two bucks apiece.

Fringe-area clergy and self-styled evangelists railed about the ATF or called down God's wrath on the holed-up cultists. A ragged, bearded man wearing blue jeans and cowboy boots, with a crown of thorns on his head, held signs in each hand. One advised, JESUS LOVES YOU. The other had a crude drawing of a pointing finger and directed, SINNERS NOTICE. THIS WAY TO MOUNT CARNAL.

Pilgrims walked to Waco from other states, lugging homemade wooden crosses and calling for understanding and a peaceful solution to the standoff. A fortune-teller with a colorful bandanna tied around her head and a crystal ball set up business outside one of the barricades. A man identifying himself as Christ Didymus Thomas showed up and told bemused reporters he was Jesus' twin brother. Thomas said he was from Orlando, Florida (the home of Disney World) and bore the scars of a crucifixion.

Jeannie Bowman passed out leaflets from a group called the Common Sense Patrol, drawing a parallel between the ATF's assault on Ranch

Apocalypse and General Santa Anna's attack on the Alamo.

Talking with the press in a vacant lot, Linda Thompson complained that the ATF was stomping on the rights of citizens to bear arms. Dressed in fatigues and armed with an AR-15 semiautomatic assault rifle, the Indianapolis lawyer called on authorities to allow the press into the compound. And she demanded that her organization, American Justice Federal, be allowed to take an inventory inside the compound after the conclusion of the standoff.

Young people wearing blue jeans, boots, and ten-gallon hats parked as near as they could get in pickup trucks and sipped at cool cans of Bud or Lone Star while lazily watching for action. Angry men in camouflage fatigues drove up on Harley-Davidsons to grump about the ATF and "government big shots poking their noses where they ain't wanted."

One day several people rode up to the checkpoint near the compound in an old-fashioned stagecoach pulled by a brace of horses. They were visiting friends in the area and had swung by the compound for a peek.

Tourists, including scores of college students on spring break, made side trips to Waco from South Padre Island, Dallas, Houston, and San Antonio to witness the action on the mid-Texas plains. Some peered past the barricades toward the compound with binoculars rented from enterprising residents of the area. Members of a wide variety of other cults caught flights or drove to Waco, to observe the operation and to take advantage of any possible opportunities to evangelize.

A slender man identifying himself as Eddie D. McTwoHats advised anyone who cared to listen that he had composed a tune he called "A Song to David." He talked about the song bringing a peaceful end to the siege.

Louis Ray Beam, Jr., got himself kicked out of a press conference at the Waco Convention Center after asking ATF Deputy Director Dan Conroy if the standoff wasn't signaling the emergence of a police state. "I won't even address answering that question," Conroy responded. When Beam attempted to attend a later briefing after being told he wasn't welcome, he was reportedly accused of criminal trespass.

An organization called the Cause Foundation, representing the former Ku Klux Grand Dragon from Houston and the *Jubilee*, a religious magazine published in California for which Beam writes, filed a $550,000 lawsuit against Waco police and the Texas Rangers. An accompanying request for a court order directing authorities to allow Beam to attend subsequent news briefings was turned down. Beam was once on the FBI's Ten Most Wanted list and was acquitted on charges of conspiring to overthrow the government.

Incredible as it appeared, nearly a month into the siege, a young man ambled through the barricades and past a small army of law officers, then dashed up to the buildings in the compound. He peeked through a couple of windows, then knocked on the door, and was admitted by the startled cultists.

The visitor who so cavalierly penetrated police lines was identified as twenty-four-year-old Louis Anthony Alaniz of Houston. Special Agent Ricks said Alaniz's mother had described her son as a religious fanatic. Word was sent to the FBI from the compound that Koresh was giving Alaniz religious instruction.

The startling feat was repeated a few days later by a slender man with long hair and a full beard who broke through the police lines and made it up to the front door of the main building. After recovering from the surprise, the Branch Davidians admitted him inside.

Ten days later, after spending his fortieth birthday with the Branch Davidians, the second intruder, who identified himself as Jesse Amen, left the compound. He told officers who debriefed him that he was a migrant fruit picker and odd jobs man, and his father's name was Lord Lightning Amen. An FBI spokesman said Amen didn't make any sense at all, no matter what they talked about, and nothing helpful was learned about the cultists during the debriefing. Amen, who claimed Koresh had washed his feet for him, was locked in the McLennan County Jail on charges of interfering with the duties of a police officer.

The demonstration of how porous the police lines around the compound were was a huge embarrassment to the FBI and other law enforcement agencies. The ATF was still taking flak over the botched raid and facing investigations. Senior FBI officials had no desire to wind up in a similar predicament. Razor wire was strung around the compound. Helicopter patrols were also stepped up to watch for intruders.

Police finally caught a reputed would-be infiltrator when a helicopter swooped down and Texas state troopers swarmed over a twenty-year-old Texas State Tech student who reputedly ignored police orders and darted into a brushy area carrying a lighted cigarette and a bottle of beer. He was arrested on charges of interfering with a law officer.

A few weeks later a South Bend, Indiana, man was taken into custody on preliminary charges of interfering with the duties of public servants after he and another man pulling handcarts full of food and other goods had a confrontation with guards at a checkpoint. They said they wanted the goods delivered to the women and children inside the compound. In Indiana, his father-in-law told the press that Gary Spaulding had gone to Texas to help the women and children because he believed they needed the same kind of aid provided to other prisoners of war.

As events surrounding the standoff increasingly took on the look of a circus, the FBI and ATF were absorbed in the serious business of trying to end the siege without further bloodshed. Negotiators were especially eager to get the children out of the compound before another outbreak of violence.

During the early hours of the siege, Koresh permitted some of the children, as well as several adults, to leave the compound individually and in small groups. By the end of the first day, ten children had been freed. Then the cult leader, speaking as if he were still in pain, announced he would surrender the compound if the electronic media broadcast a prerecorded message. The FBI kept its word, and his fifty-five-minute sermon was broadcast on radio and television.

But Koresh broke his word. Instead of surrendering himself and everyone else in the compound, he released seven more children and two women. He also revealed for the first time how many people were inside: forty-three men, forty-seven women, and twenty children. He was believed to have fathered most of the children who still hadn't been freed.

The cult leader put the blame for the lie on a higher power. "God told me to wait," he said, explaining that the Deity had instructed him to hold off for a divine message before surrendering. Koresh's announcement led to speculation among cult experts and former Branch Davidians that he was referring either to a celestial sign or to a fire, earthquake, storm, or other natural disaster.

The electronic media had assumed a unique role in the siege, but their intrusion into the talks was a mixed blessing. Approximately forty-eight hours after the gunfight, senior officials at the scene cut the telephone lines the cultists were using to talk to the press. It was a new ball game. If Koresh or his second-in-command, Steve Schneider, wanted to talk with someone on the outside, they had to talk with a government negotiator. There were several, and they worked in shifts, around the clock.

A specially trained mediator was assigned to the roles of primary contact and father confessor. It was his task to attempt to develop a trusting relationship with Koresh. The point man was backed by a colleague who listened to every conversation and used his knowledge and skills to prompt the agent on the phone. It was his job as well to guard against the primary contact becoming too emotionally tied to the cultist.

Both negotiators were backed by a coach, who was responsible for coordinating the operation and deciding what information should be related to the primary contact and the backup.

It was a carefully thought-out, proven system staffed by trained professionals; it had worked before; and it was the best negotiation tool available at that time. But each incident was different, and no one claimed the system was perfect.

Jeffrey Jamar was well trained and experienced, but he was traveling an incredibly difficult road that was filled with potholes and hazards of all kinds. Negotiating with a religious zealot who believed he had a direct pipeline to God's on-the-scene advice, who was armed to the teeth, and who was backed by a band of fanatic followers who had already demonstrated their willingness to martyr themselves for their leader was a near-impossible task.

For one thing, negotiators were quickly learning that Koresh had a loose interpretation of God's commandment against bearing false witness. He was a liar! Dropouts from the cult explained that he taught his followers it was perfectly acceptable to lie to unbelievers.

Negotiators were also frustrated because they were unable to learn the true number of fatalities and injuries among the Ranch Apocalypse defenders. They suspected there were many more deaths than Koresh had conceded during his statements directly after the shoot-out.

Eventually Steve Schneider turned over to the FBI the names of six cultists he claimed had been killed in the firefight. Listed among the dead along with Peter Gent and Michael Schroeder were Winston Blake; Koresh's father-in-law, Perry Jones; Peter Hipsman, the twenty-eight-year-old son of a New York fireman; and Jaydone Wendell, the thirty-four-year-old daughter of a retired officer from the Honolulu Police Department.

The FBI had no means of confirming the toll, and the press variously reported numbers ranging from three or four to twenty-five dead inside the compound.

Authorities were also concerned about injured cultists who might need professional medical care. Steve Schneider's wife, Judith, whom Koresh had inducted into the House of David, was wounded in the shoulder and right hand during the shoot-out. One of her fingers was badly infected and believed to be becoming gangrenous.

Two physicians talked to the cultists by telephone and informed authorities that if the finger wasn't properly treated she might die. Mrs. Schneider suggested she might simply cut the finger off. The doctor she was talking to told her that solution was "barbaric."

The FBI refused to send doctors into the compound, but stressed that medical care would be made available as soon as the holdouts surrendered. "Our goal is not to treat everybody in there and make them happy," Ricks told reporters. "Our goal is to get them out."

Adults and children released from the compound either gave conflicting stories about deaths and injuries or simply didn't know.

Although Koresh continued to sidestep government pleas to end the siege and allow the courts to sort things out, he released additional cultists, a few at a time. One day two children were released; the next day one child left the compound. As the children were driven away by federal agents they ran a gauntlet of reporters and photographers, all clamoring to ask questions or snap photographs.

None of the children was injured, and all were clean and appeared to have been well cared for. Several of them carried notes with their names and such information as ages, as well as messages written to grandparents or other relatives.

Two of the first children released carried a box full of puppies with them. Their mother was the Alsatian killed during the gun battle.

At the request of the ATF's Sharon Wheeler, several television and radio stations broadcast notes about the puppies, pointing out that they needed homes. A few minutes after the plea was broadcast, all twelve were adopted, and telephones were still ringing from would-be foster parents.

The youngsters were spirited away to a shelter provided by the Texas Child Protective Services Department, where they were fed, permitted to watch television cartoons, read children's books, and talk with child care professionals and mental health experts about their fears and emotional reactions to the firefight. Several of the children told about hiding under beds as gunfire ripped through the ramshackle walls of the compound.

Therapists publicly cautioned that the children might carry the emotional scars of their trauma for years. Before every meal or sit-down snack, the children immediately joined hands and prayed, workers noticed. Nonetheless, some clergymen and theological scholars expressed concern that Koresh's twisted use of the Scriptures on the youngsters might turn them against all religion and make it difficult for them to believe in anything.

After a few days, most of the youngsters were placed in temporary foster families, sent to the local Methodist Home for Children, or assigned to short-time shelters.

Several of the freed adults were in their sixties or seventies, and only a few healthy young men walked from the compound. None of the freed cultists was injured in the gunfight, although one woman was hospitalized with a previously existing medical condition. Fifty-nine-year-old Victorine Hollingsworth was treated for heart trouble and high blood pressure. Ms. Hollingsworth was from England. Other cultists were from countries as disparate as New Zealand, Canada, Israel, the Philippines, and Guyana. Koresh had attracted a rainbow mix of nationalities and races.

Most of the adults were initially taken to the McLennan County Jail and held on a variety of charges or as material witnesses. Many of them were later released, however, some to a Salvation Army shelter in Waco or to other halfway houses.

As the siege dragged on, the government replaced the Bradley M2AOs with more heavily armored Abrams M1 tanks from Fort Hood. During the talks, the cultists had threatened to open fire again.

The military vehicles were used to clear cars and rubble from the perimeter in order to eliminate possible cover for snipers or cult gunmen. The *Tribune-Herald* company car left behind by England during the firefight was flattened when government agents used one of the Bradleys to push it off a road it was blocking. Ricks responded to complaints from newspaper executives by explaining that the government agents weren't professional drivers of armored military vehicles. The government suggested the matter could wait to be sorted out after the siege ended.

Weeks later, a much fancier, more expensive car parked next to the compound was also banged up by a student driver using an armored vehicle to clear the area near the buildings. It was Koresh's shiny black Camaro, which he tinkered with at the Mag Bag and occasionally used to take favored disciples on rides. The cult leader whined about missing his car during some of the on-again, off-again talks with FBI negotiators.

Once, as federal agents were shifting equipment around, cultists held children up to the windows. FBI agents were unsure if they were merely being given a chance to watch what was going on, or if they were being used as human shields.

Sharpshooters from the FBI's Hostage Rescue Team were watching the windows around the clock, and several times they had Koresh in the cross hairs of their gunsights. They weren't ready to bypass the courts, however, and they didn't shoot. After the brief skirmish in front of the compound a few hours after the main firefight, the nearly five hundred law officers surrounding the compound never fired a single shot throughout the remainder of the siege.

The cultists also revealed that Melissa Morrison, a six-year-old girl from England, wanted to leave. Soon after that, however, they claimed that the girl, whose mother, Rosemary, was also inside, had changed her mind. The number of children released from the compound continued to stand at twenty-nine.

In Waco, District Court Judge Bill Loque ordered all but three of the children released by the cultists to remain in temporary state custody. The other three were turned over to their father, Air Force Sergeant William Mabb. The sergeant was permanently stationed at Ellsworth Air Force Base in South Dakota. But he flew to Texas from the island of Guam where he was on temporary duty, and obtained an emergency custody order from the courts. Sergeant Mabb returned to his base with his children. Their younger half brother, whose father was fatally wounded in the skirmish outside the compound, remained in CPS custody. His mother was permitted to visit with him.

The children's thirty-four-year-old mother, Kathryn Schroeder, was one of the cultists who had left the compound. An FBI spokesman said she'd left because she wanted to be reunited with her three-year-old son, Brian.

A native of Tampa, Florida, Kathryn had married Mabb in 1982 when both were in the air force and she filed for divorce three years later. She was given custody of the children, and after marrying Schroeder, she moved with her family to Miami. The couple first met Koresh there, and in 1989 they sold their possessions and moved with the children to the compound outside Waco.

Other children were later released to relatives after screening by child welfare authorities and the courts. Among the first children to leave were three-year-old Crystal and six-year-old Angelica Sonobe, whose parents, Scott and Floracita Sonobe, remained inside the compound. The girls were released to the custody of their grandfather, Ken Sonobe, on Oahu in Hawaii.

Livingston Fagan and Sheila Martin also surrendered to authorities. Mrs. Martin's four younger children were released as well, but her attorney husband, Douglas, and their three older sons, twenty-one, eighteen, and fifteen years old, stayed behind.

Other relatives, including Kathy Jones, continued to seek custody of the remaining children who had been freed. When Mrs. Jones's nine-year-old daughter, Heather, left the compound, she carried a gift certificate and a bag of clothes given to her by one of her roommates, Judith Schneider. The girl was accompanied out of the compound by her eleven- and twelve-year-old brothers, Kevin and Mark.

As the number of children leaving the compound rose to nearly thirty, child protection employees appealed for volunteers from their thirty-county CPS region to help out in Waco. The volunteers were asked to take over the regular caseloads of workers assigned to the children from the compound. CPS caseworkers joined ATF, FBI, and other law enforcement officers ringing the compound during the twenty-four-hour-a-day vigil, to ensure that professionals would be on hand if additional children were released.

The cultists hung a banner outside one of the buildings, reading: GOD HELP US. WE WANT THE PRESS. It was the first of various banners the Branch Davidians would hang outside compound buildings. The day after calling for the press, they hung a banner asking to talk with the

Constitution Foundational Association and Don Stewart. Based in Richland Hills just outside of Fort Worth, the fledgling organization claimed it was concerned about protecting the constitutional rights of the holed-up cultists.

The CFA wasn't called on by the FBI for help, but negotiations weren't going well. Koresh wasn't a man who kept his word, and it was difficult for negotiators to keep up with his confounding mood swings and broken promises. At one point he agreed to fill three buses with about thirty Branch Davidians who wanted to leave, and permit them to exit from the compound. After the buses pulled up near the main doors of the compound, Koresh told the government agents to wait because he had to use the bathroom. He never returned, and eventually the buses were driven away, empty. The fickle cult leader had lied, or changed his mind.

Sheriff Harwell stepped into the negotiations to see if he could pull off a repeat of his performance a few years earlier and talk Koresh into peacefully surrendering. Eventually, the sheriff and Jamar both signed a letter that was hand-delivered to the compound promising Koresh that if he surrendered he could talk with his followers in jail and would be given airtime on the Christian Broadcasting Network. Although the cult leader had previously indicated interest in the offer, he ignored the letter and allowed a deadline to pass without a reply.

The sixty-four-year-old sheriff, who slept most nights in a tent at the siege site, became the first negotiator who wasn't a federal law enforcement officer. But he wouldn't be the last. Clergymen, Branch Davidian dropouts, and experts from around the country with experience dealing with cults and with deprogramming contacted the FBI offering their help in negotiations. During the first week of the siege, nearly two thousand calls were logged by federal agencies, the McLennan County Sheriff's Department, and the Waco Police Department from people with ideas about how the Koreshians could be lured outside, and from self-styled Bible scholars volunteering their interpretations of the cult leader's confusing religious ramblings. Calls were logged from almost every state as well as China, South Africa, Israel, England, Canada, and other countries. Most of the callers indicated they believed Koresh was correct in predicting that the end of the world was just around the corner. Other would-be go-betweens telephoned or wrote to radio stations and newspapers with tips for bringing the barricaded cultists outside.

Author-evangelist-pastor Mike Evans was quoted in the *Fort Worth Star-Telegram* as offering to enter the compound and cast out a demon he was convinced had taken possession of the cult leader. If that wasn't permitted, said the Euless, Texas, Assembly of God preacher, they could simply use loudspeakers set up in front of the compound to broadcast a prayer rebuking the demon inside Koresh and commanding it to leave in the name of Jesus. The Reverend Evans said the speaker had to be turned up loud and the prayers repeatedly chanted for the exorcism to work.

The pleas of Jean Holub, Koresh's grand-mother, for permission to enter the compound were rejected. She later delivered a package to a senior ATF agent for Koresh, containing a tape recording from his father of a telephone conver-sation with a Houston lawyer Bobby Howell had hired for his son. Balenda Ganem and members of other families also pleaded unsuccessfully to be permitted to talk with the barricaded cultists. The cult experts and the family members were not given major roles in the negotiations. But eventually lawyers were.

The standoff had barely begun before lawyers were seeking access to the barricaded cultists. The morning after the shoot-out, Gary Coker, Jr., telephoned his fellow attorney, Douglas Martin, inside the compound to tell him about a movie offer from a producer in California. The lawyer reasoned that it might help to appeal to the cult leader's ego by pointing out that if he stayed alive he would have some control over a movie about him. If Koresh was dead, he wouldn't have any control. And few people, if any, would argue that the self-proclaimed Messiah was a person who didn't like to be in control.

But it was the third week of the siege before letters from lawyers were included in a package sent into the compound. The package also included some audiotapes and copies of national magazines Koresh had asked for. The magazines had articles about the Branch Davidians and Koresh's photo on the covers. Later, the FBI sent in milk for the children and medical supplies.

During one or more of the deliveries to the compound, the FBI smuggled tiny transmitters and listening devices into the headquarters. Sensitive surveillance equipment that detects body heat then helped agents keep tabs on the movement of cult members inside. Forward-looking infrared systems developed for military surveillance and known by the acronym FLIRS were trained on outer doors to keep watch for possible nocturnal activity by the cultists.

A few weeks into the siege, Attorney Dick DeGuerin stepped firmly into the picture. The intense fifty-two-year-old lawyer was hired by Koresh's mother to represent her son. He made several trips into the compound, first by himself, then with another attorney, to talk about the Branch Davidians' legal options and other matters in an effort to bring a peaceful solution to the crisis. DeGuerin stressed to reporters, however, that he should not be considered a negotiator.

The first time DeGuerin was allowed to meet with the holdouts, he rode up to the compound on a motorcycle and knocked on the door. One of the cult members emerged, and they shook hands while the small army of law enforcement officers watched from a few yards away. After the greeting the cultist went back inside the building, returned with a chair, then went inside once more. The lawyer took off his jacket, sat down, and began talking—apparently with someone on the other side of the door.

The Houston attorney was already well known in the Waco area for his defense in the retrial of Muneer Deeb, who was convicted in 1985 and sentenced to death for allegedly setting up the contract murder that led to the slaying of the three teenagers at Lake Waco. DeGuerin's spirited defense won an acquittal for Deeb, the most recent in a series of clients he had represented who were tied to highly publicized Texas homicides.

FBI Special Agent Bob Ricks told reporters that even though DeGuerin would become an opponent of the government after the siege ended, the negotiators were wishing him success. Ricks was the bureau's senior spokesman in Waco.

DeGuerin's new high-profile role signaled an important turnaround for the government. They had flatly refused his previous efforts to get into the compound, maintaining that the holdouts weren't entitled to confer with lawyers because they hadn't been taken into custody. Government lawyers had appeared in federal court and successfully held off the efforts of defense attorneys to meet with the cultists.

Even after approving DeGuerin's meeting with the Branch Davidians, Ricks made it plain that the government wasn't about to send a lawyer into the compound for each cult member. "We do not want to get in a situation where we have one hundred different attorneys going into that compound," he declared.

Nevertheless, DeGuerin's entry onto the scene called for some cautious legal tightrope walking and seemed to raise questions about the role of defense attorneys in similar situations. Foremost was defining his responsibilities as Koresh's legal adviser, balanced against efforts to mediate a peaceful resolution. Even a slight error in DeGuerin's legal judgment might lead to criminal charges or trouble with the bar association.

The lawyer had to be extremely careful of the advice he offered.

DeGuerin's insertion into the wheeling and dealing with Koresh didn't mark the first time that a lawyer had sought to mediate a standoff involving federal law enforcment officers. In 1987, attorney Gary Leshaw walked into the Atlanta penitentiary to talk with Cuban prisoners holding ninety-four hostages. The confrontation was eventually mediated when an eight-point agreement was reached with federal officials and the hostages were released after eleven days.

Celebrity attorney Melvin Belli of San Francisco created a mild stir when he announced he had been hired to represent Koresh and asked permission to have an associate meet with the holed-up Branch Davidian leader. Belli said he was retained by Mrs. Holub and a Florida lawyer, Gary Hunt. Belli's representative claimed that a radio talk-show host had asked whether the cultists wanted Hunt to represent them, and they had jiggled their TV satellite dish. That, it was claimed, was a signal giving power of attorney for Koresh to the Florida lawyer. Hunt subsequently passed on the authority to Belli. The FBI responded to the convoluted explanation by turning down the request.

In Waco, other attorneys were also moving into the picture as they were contacted for help by relatives of the cultists. DeGuerin, however, continued to command the spotlight. With FBI approval, Houston lawyer Jack B. Zimmermann talked by telephone with Schneider, Koresh's right-hand man. Filling in for his injured leader, Schneider was taking a major role in the drawn-out and frustrating negotiations. Occasionally, Martin also participated in talks.

Zimmermann told reporters that mistrust of the government agents and concern over treatment after leaving the compound were major roadblocks preventing a solution to the crisis. He said he and DeGuerin were attempting to assure the Branch Davidians "that we are on their side, that we are their lawyers, that their interest in the courtroom is our interest," and that their legal rights would be protected.

At a press conference after one of the palavers between DeGuerin, Zimmermann, and the cultists, the lawyers revealed that Koresh and his followers had agreed to leave the compound following the observance of Passover. DeGuerin said they were more convinced than ever that there would be a peaceful resolution. "There is not going to be a violent end, at least as far as David is concerned. There's not going to be anybody hurt. They're ready for this to be over, but they have a very important agenda. Their agenda is the observance of Passover."

Neither of the lawyers would cite a specific day the cultists would surrender, however. "Right now they believe there is a higher law that they must follow," Zimmermann said. "Were we not on the eve of Passover, they'd be out by now."

There was a long history among the Branch Davidians of important events being associated with Passover. The Living Prophet's devastating message about the New Light was one. Current and former members of the cult had also revealed that Koresh had talked of the 1993 Passover as being the last they would observe together.

The lawyers reported working out a specific surrender plan that had DeGuerin and Koresh walking out of the compound together first. After it was demonstrated to Koresh's followers that it was safe to come out, they would follow. Zimmermann and Schneider would be the last of the approximately ninety people to leave.

The lawyers had other intriguing stories to tell as well. The cultists said they were fired on from helicopters during the assault on the compound. And they claimed they had taken four ATF agents captive during the shoot-out, then released them. The ATF firmly denied that either claim was true.

One more apparent untruth was disclosed

when the lawyers said they were unaware of any children killed or injured during the clash. Koresh, it seemed, had lied in the radio report claiming that his two-year-old daughter had died in the assault.

As negotiations continued near Waco, in New York a pair of Park Avenue lawyers were sending faxes to book publishers asking for bids on Koresh's story. Michael Kennedy and Kenneth Burrows claimed a floor of $2.5 million in the rights auction. According to a story in the *New York Times*, the faxes stated the attorneys had been retained as the exclusive agents for Koresh and for his lawyer, DeGuerin, on book, television, and movie deals. CNN broadcast a similar story about the reported effort to sell book, television, and movie rights to Koresh's story.

Government spokesmen echoed the optimism of the lawyers that the approaching Passover holiday might lead to a resolution of the standoff. And they agreed to the lawyers' plan to escort their clients out of the compound during the surrender, whenever it occurred. But they didn't ease off on their own efforts to negotiate a surrender, and to keep the psychological pressure on.

Soon after the standoff began, government forces shut off the cult's electricity. The cultists lit the interior of the dark buildings at night with lanterns. The government began shining trailer-mounted spotlights on the compound throughout the night and serenaded them with highly amplified recorded music and messages. The most chilling recording was a statement by Koresh claiming he was ready to do battle all over again, to fulfill prophecies by dying in a holy war.

"If they want blood, then our blood is here for them to shed. . . . We are not afraid of the government. If we have to die for what we stand for, we're going to. I don't mind if I die." FBI negotiators wanted to make sure cultists inside the fortress knew what their leader was saying.

Avoiding rock and roll, heavy metal, or any other music Koresh could be expected to favor, the agents chose their serenades from an eclectic selection of music and noise. They played everything from the shrill shrieks of rabbits being slaughtered and the sounds of dental drills, to Tibetan Buddhist chants, marches, reveille, Christmas carols, and Nancy Sinatra's 1960s pop hit "These Boots Were Made for Walkin'." Koresh, however, didn't take the hint and put on his boots to walk out.

The blaring music and noise was a psychological warfare technique that had been utilized in the past. The best-known instance was when Panamanian dictator Manuel Noriega was holed up in the papal nuncio's headquarters in Panama City and the U.S. Army blasted loud music outside the compound until he gave up.

Earlier, the FBI had informed Koresh they'd had their fill of his convoluted scriptural ramblings and set new rules. They would only discuss substantive matters related to ending the standoff. The FBI wasn't there to be converted, a senior agent remarked to the media. Negotiators tightened the screws, increasing pressure in an effort to make a breakthrough. The cultists responded by producing another banner calling for talks with the news media. They also began tapping out Morse code messages with a flashing light beamed on a window after dark. "SOS, SOS, SOS, SOS, FBI broke negotiations. We want negotiations from press," the message declared.

Direct communication between the FBI and the cultists dipped into a lull. During a period of a few days, only Sheriff Harwell and a couple of cultists recently freed from the compound had managed telephone conversations with the barricaded Branch Davidians. Most people outside the compound were still calling them that, although one of the freed cult members reported that they wanted to be called by their new name, Koreshians.

Koresh and his followers were increasingly

difficult to deal with, while negotiators patiently wrestled with his outlandish claims and demands. Negotiators were also given crash courses in the books of Revelation and Daniel by knowledgeable theologians. That may have helped, but it didn't solve the problem. Koresh had developed his own curiously warped theology.

"What we have right now confronting us is that we are required to prove that David is not Christ, which is an impossible task," Ricks said at a press briefing.

"I don't believe there's anybody out there in the world that can prove to his satisfaction that he's not Christ. When you're God, it's very difficult to have someone come forward and prove you're not God."

Negotiators were becoming increasingly frustrated by the seesaw haggling and extremely worried about the welfare of the cultists, especially the children, inside the slapped-together fortification. At least two of the women, including Aisha Gyarfas, were pregnant. But Koresh continued to talk about a violent ending to the affair, an Apocalypse.

There was brief hope that a small earthquake that occurred in mid-April might be interpreted by Koresh as the sign from God. But it occurred deep in southern Texas, and the cult leader apparently decided it was too far away to be God's signal. Koresh's grandmother, Jean Holub, also tried to lure him out by telling him in an audiotape that her presence at the site was the sign he was waiting for from God.

"Now, Vernon, you need to come on out just as soon as I'm sure you and the others won't be attacked or mistreated," she pleaded. She said she didn't believe she would be there if the "good Lord" didn't mean her presence to be a sign he wanted the siege ended.

Koresh didn't come out. Instead, he began sending threatening letters to the law officers, picking out darkly allegorical bits and pieces from Revelation and other books of the Bible. He appeared to be careening away from reality and deeper into the ominous apocalyptic morass of doom and destruction. He signed one of the letters "Yahweh Koresh." Yahweh is a form of the Hebrew name for God.

In the first letter he warned that an earthquake was going to rock the area and break open cracks in a dam on Lake Waco. "Learn from David my seals, or, as you have said, bear the consequences," it cautioned. "I forewarn you that the Lake Waco area of Old Mount Carmel will be terribly shaken. The waters of the lake will be emptied through the broken dam. The heavens are calling you to judgement."

The threat led to fears that cultists or sympathizers on the outside might attempt to damage either the Lake Waco dam or another dam on Lake Brazos. Schneider assured the FBI, however, that Koresh was referring to a natural disaster, not sabotage.

Schneider was permitted to emerge from the compound to deliver the second note and to light seven smoke flares as part of the cult's observance of Good Friday, which they considered a high holy day. When Schneider emerged one more time than anticipated, officers "flash-banged" him, tossing concussion grenades designed to stun and disorient him.

The second letter was reportedly dictated in the first person by Koresh to Judy Schneider, who wrote it down. It was even more menacing than the first, and angrily warned against harming Koresh. The four-page note was written as if an all-powerful God were speaking through the cult leader. There were dark references to authorities being "devoured by fire or destroyed by other means."

DeGuerin interpreted the letters more optimistically, claiming that some of the phrases might instead mean that his client was looking forward to telling his story and exacting retribution against his enemy, the ATF, in the courts.

It was obvious to most people, however, that

Koresh and other lead negotiators within the compound were showing increasing signs of militant paranoia. They were behaving as if they believed they were dealing with demonic forces.

Signals being sent by the cultists were growing ever more ominous, and they had stopped releasing children. Authorities believed that as many as seventeen youngsters ten years old or younger were still inside. Koresh apparently had fathered many of them, including the son and daughter, Cyrus and Star, he'd had with his wife, Rachel.

There were warnings outside the compound as well:

- Breault was quoted by the *Tribune-Herald* saying that, based on what he knew of Koresh's beliefs, the cultists might be expecting the standoff to end in their deaths. But after about three months they would be resurrected and take a terrible retribution on the unbelievers. It was a chilling thought.
- During her appearance on *Donahue*, Kiri Jewell urged government forces to invade the compound, even if it led to the death of some of the occupants. "Better a few people die than all of them," the girl reasoned.
- The Branch Davidians had been flying their cult flag, a Star of David on a blue field,

since the day after the shoot-out. Cult experts warned that it might be Koresh's notice that he was establishing Mount Zion, from which God's chosen would be lifted to heaven.

• Coker and former cultists had worriedly pointed out that Koresh was thirty-three. That was the same age as Christ when he was martyred on the cross. But Christ died a singular death and didn't take his apostles with him. Judging from what was known of the barricaded cult leader who claimed to be the new Messiah, he wasn't expected to endure his personal Calvary alone.

• Ricks also publicly cautioned that Koresh might be planning mass suicide, despite the cult leader's earlier denials to negotiators. Koresh had taught his followers that as the Lamb of God, "he has to be slain and there has to be a sufficient number of martyrs— those of his followers who also have to be slain—before you have a complete fulfillment of the prophecies," the FBI spokesman declared.

Koresh lied about surrendering after the Passover holiday. Instead, he devised a new story for the attorneys and government negotiators. He tantalized government negotiators with the possibility of a peaceful settlement. DeGuerin reported that his client was prepared to surrender after completing work on a tract explaining the seven seals and the apocalyptic prophecies surrounding them. "David has been working day and night, composing a manuscript that will be delivered to me, upon which he will then come out," the attorney said.

DeGuerin conceded that he couldn't provide an exact time when Koresh would complete the work. But he said his client wanted two religious scholars to inspect it before the surrender. The government negotiators waited awhile, but time dragged on and there was still no manuscript, and no surrender.

They had tripped down the path of broken promises with Koresh before, and hardly anyone believed him anymore except his loyal disciples and the lawyers who had been going into the compound. "We have had so many stalling tactics over such a long period of time we are not that overly optimistic," said FBI spokesman Richard Swenson.

Ricks's response was on target but more sarcastic. "It's like that *Peanuts* cartoon—Is Lucy going to pull that football out one more time?" he asked. He observed that the high school dropout was a poor writer, and even after completing the tract it would have to be edited by Schneider.

Koresh was batting 0 for 3 with his promises to surrender the compound, Ricks pointed out. He had lied about surrendering after the radio broadcast; he had lied when he promised on March 19 to give up by the next day or within a month; and he hadn't backed up his lawyer, who told authorities on March 31 "in no uncertain terms" that the siege would end after the Passover holiday.

The FBI spokesman added that Koresh had a big ego and, based on his letters, wasn't concerned about anyone but himself. The cult leader didn't mention any of his companions in the letters, the agent said, only himself.

Ricks denied news reports that the White House continued to fear further bloodshed and was turning thumbs down on schemes to force an end to the violence. Patience and time were running out.

Government authorities quietly began setting into motion a carefully conceived plan to turn up the pressure another notch. This time they would use tanks and tear gas. No one among the approximately five hundred law officers and other professionals ringing the compound wanted more martyrs—on either side.

# CHAPTER NINE

# The Apocalypse

FAINT HINTS OF LIGHT CREEPING OVER THE eastern horizon had just begun to silhouette the low boxlike shapes of the buildings at Ranch Apocalypse when Byron Sage made his final telephone call to the barricaded cultists.

It was 5:59 on Monday morning April 19, the fifty-first day of the siege, and the FBI's forty-three-year-old chief negotiator told Steve Schneider the government was through waiting. Armored vehicles were going to begin tearing chunks out of the buildings and pumping in tear gas.

As Sage began reading from a carefully prepared statement, Schneider interrupted. "You're going to gas us?" he gasped. The cultist was disbelieving, stunned by the news. He clicked off the telephone, ripped the line from the wall, and chucked it out a window.

Sage, the white-haired, bespectacled leader of a thirty-member FBI negotiating team, who had camped outside the compound for all but one day of the standoff, never talked with any of the cultists inside Ranch Apocalypse again.

Inside and outside the barricaded fortress, the die was cast!

The decision to make a move to break the frustrating standoff had been carefully considered and planned. Members of the FBI's famous psychological profile team, which was so highly publicized through the book and movie *The Silence of the Lambs*, had been called in to study Koresh. The profile worked up by the team of experts indicated he wasn't likely to commit suicide or lead his followers in mass self-destruction.

Throughout the siege, one of the main concerns of the government forces ringing the compound and in Washington, D.C., was the fear that Koresh might emulate the mad preacher Jim Jones, who had led nine hundred of his followers to their deaths in Guyana.

The team of experts had based part of their

judgment on what they believed was Koresh's unwillingness to suffer more physical pain or die. At one point he had schemed to booby-trap himself with hand grenades before walking outside as if to parley with or surrender to federal agents so that he could blow them up along with himself. Koresh had met with his followers in the chapel, said goodbye to his disciples, and kissed his children. Then, Ricks later disclosed at a press conference, he had "chickened out."

During one of his talks with Sage, the cult leader said suicide conflicted with his religious beliefs. "I'm too young to die in here," he added.

Statements by DeGuerin and cult members who had left the compound also backed up the conclusion that Koresh and his followers were unlikely to commit suicide. Most senior FBI agents and other government officials involved in the affair believed the increasingly frustrating stalemate could be resolved without precipitating another Guyana-type mass suicide or murder.

That assessment was passed on to Attorney General Janet Reno when the FBI's plan was presented to her a week before Sage made his final telephone call to the barricaded cultists. The proposal called for shrinking the perimeter of the compound and increasing the discomfort of the holdouts by ripping chunks out of some of the buildings and filling them with tear gas.

FBI experts believed use of the gas would be one of the best ways of staving off a mass suicide because it would create so much confusion and disorder inside the compound.

The attorney general had been on the job as the nation's top law enforcement officer only a few weeks when the plan was dropped into her lap. She studied it for almost a week, looking at the plan from both logistical and human angles. Like the federal, state, and local law enforcement officers ringing the compound and providing support services, she wanted the siege brought to a conclusion without further bloodshed.

Negotiations with the barricaded cultists were not bearing fruit. They had enough food to hold out for another year or more, and surveillance had disclosed they were continuing to build up their fortifications and were constructing additional gun ports. Bales of hay were stacked along inside walls.

On Saturday night, April 17, the attorney general met with senior FBI officials and top aides to make a decision on the plan. She had carefully considered the various options presented to her by experts and advisers familiar with the situation. There weren't many options to study, and most of those that were available for consideration weren't very attractive.

Some consideration had been given to constructing a wall around Ranch Apocalypse so that the police vigil could be continued with greatly reduced manpower. But authorities were worried about the safety of construction teams, who could be fired on by the barricaded cultists.

Pulling back and waiting for another year or so to starve the cultists out simply wasn't practical.

And an all-out frontal assault was almost certain to lead to a bloodbath worse than the slaughter nearly two months earlier.

One of the attorney general's overriding concerns, a Justice Department spokesman later explained, was protecting from physical harm the roughly two dozen children known still to be inside Ranch Apocalypse. Too many reports of serious child abuse had been carried out of the compound to be ignored. She was also worried that the children might suffer from disease caused by the deteriorating sanitation, the buildup of human waste, and the possible presence of long-dead bodies within the compound.

After questioning the FBI during telephone calls between Texas and Washington about the effects of the tear gas on children, the attorney general gave her permission to turn up the pressure. She also directed that ambulances were to be standing by at the compound when the assault began. Twelve doctors, dozens of medical technicians, and a Red Cross mobile unit were brought into place.

When Jeffrey Jamar was notified of the go-ahead,

he was making a brief visit to his family in San Antonio. The Austin native and twenty-four-year FBI career man returned to Waco the next day to begin putting the operation in motion.

The same day, less than twenty-four hours before the assault, Attorney General Reno talked once more with President Clinton about the plan to turn up the pressure on the cultists.

"Now, I want you to tell me once more why you believe—not why they [the FBI] believe—why you believe we should move now rather than wait some more," he asked.

Because of the children, the president later told a news conference she replied. Reno reportedly told him the evidence indicated that they were still being abused, and conditions inside the compound were becoming increasingly unsafe.

Clinton gave her the green light.

Inside Ranch Apocalypse on Monday morning, as soon as the telephone was tossed outside the cultists launched into a flurry of activity. Gas masks were distributed to men, women, and children. Mothers ran through the routine they had practiced with their children many times before, showing them how to put the masks on and breathe with them. Men and women with rifles and other weapons hurried to take places at windows, doors, and near rooftops.

A few minutes after 6:00 A.M., an M728 combat engineering vehicle with tank treads pulled up to the main building and stopped a few feet from the south corner. A government agent inside the armored vehicle used a loudspeaker to plead with the barricaded cultists to come out:

"This is not an assault! Do not fire! Exit the compound and follow instructions," he implored.

The speaker's plea was met with a barrage of small-arms fire. Bullets slammed into the fifty-eight-ton former tank, flattened, and glanced off the armor. The M728 moved forward, smashing a ragged chunk of the wooden corner off the building.

Other armored combat vehicles lumbered into view and began chewing away huge pieces of other buildings, as the cultists met them with a heavy sheet of gunfire. At least two hundred shots were fired by the defenders, but the government agents were well protected by flak jackets and the military armor and there were no injuries. The FBI and ATF didn't return the fire.

Instead, more holes were punched through buildings with ramrods attached to the noses of the armored vehicles, and gas was pumped inside. A disabling gas commonly used to control riots and other violent demonstrations was selected largely for its nonincendiary character. It is composed of a chemical with the tongue-twisting name 0-chlorobenzylidenemalononitrile, though understandably the Defense Department and other agencies and individuals familiar with it refer to it by a shorter designation: CS.

CS is generally nonlethal, although it can be dangerous to people suffering from asthma and other respiratory diseases. By whatever name it is called, CS is extremely unpleasant. It stings eyes and flesh, makes noses run, and causes choking, dizziness, and crying.

Inside the buildings one of the cultists slipped his mask off for a moment to swallow a drink of water; he reeled back, slapping his hands to his face. His eyes, throat, and flesh felt as if they were on fire, later reports indicated.

There would be eventual disagreement over exactly how the tear gas was delivered. The government insisted a gas generator on the armored vehicle was used to turn the white CS crystals into a fine mist as it was pumped inside with compressed air. Some cultists who were in the besieged compound at the time, however, later claimed that canisters were shot inside, turning into deadly flying missiles and careening off walls.

As the armored vehicles smashed at the walls and shot gas into the flimsy buildings, Koresh scrambled down from his apartment to check the women and children on the second floor just below. He inspected their masks, shouted orders, and roamed the trembling hallways that were filling with gas, dust, and debris.

After the initial flurry of activity, some of the cult members attempted to resume their normal chores, ignoring as best they could the armored vehicles ripping away at the buildings in the complex. With their faces covered with gas masks, women tended to the children, read their Bibles, did laundry, or wandered around the kitchen trying to figure out how to prepare and serve meals.

About three hours after the assault began, a white banner was draped from an observation deck atop the main building. A message was scratched out in orange, reading, WE WANT OUR PHONES FIXED.

A few minutes after noon, six hours after the attack began, FBI snipers spotted two men apparently setting fires at the east and west edges of the compound. The cultists were dressed in black and were wearing gas masks. Agents overhead in helicopters also videotaped the fire apparently starting almost simultaneously in different locations.

Wisps of smoke began trailing upward from several locations, including second-story windows. Then flames spurted out. Immediately caught by a brisk wind gusting up to thirty miles per hour, the fire scooted across the wood frame buildings in a rush. In moments, while horrified law enforcement officers watched helplessly, the compound erupted in a volcano of flame and smoke.

Explosions added to the conflagration when stockpiles of ammunition, chemicals, or stores of incendiaries erupted, sending new fireballs tearing through the flimsy buildings. The largest of the fireballs flashed through the compound at 12:28 P.M., collapsing the watchtower.

Americans watching the assault on television sets throughout the country shared the sudden shock and horror as their screens were filled with vivid images of the conflagration. It seemed that no one inside the compound could possibly survive.

Balenda Ganem was watching television at her motel in Waco. She peered at the screen looking for fire trucks. But there weren't any. The FBI had decided it would be too risky to have fire fighters at the scene because the .50-caliber machine gun the cultists were known to have could strike targets up to three thousand yards away.

In South Bend, David Jewell was talking on the telephone with an interviewer from the Cable News Network when the fire started. One of his first thoughts when he learned of the blaze was thankfulness that his daughter, Kiri, was in school in Niles and wasn't parked in front of a television set watching the compound go up in flames.

While viewers around the nation peered at their television screens in helpless fascination, a man climbed out a window onto the roof of one of the buildings. His clothing was in flames as he tumbled off onto the ground.

Offscreen, a woman lurched and twisted through a doorway, with her clothes and body on fire. An FBI agent tackled her, but as he tried to beat out the flames she broke away and struggled back inside. Agents chased her and dragged her to safety. The heroics of rescuers were accomplished at the risk of their own lives. Not only did they have to brave the flames, but they were also at risk of being shot by surviving cultists or injured by exploding munitions.

Ricks later told interviewers that the government officers ringing the flaming compound had hoped the maternal instinct would lead women to grab up their children and run for their lives. If any of the mothers did indeed try to escape with their children, FBI and ATF agents saw no sign of their efforts.

At 12:38 P.M., about ten minutes after the huge fireball erupted, fire trucks and other emergency vehicles began arriving at Ranch Apocalypse from Waco and the nearby towns of Bellmead, Axtell, Hallsburg, and Mart. By that time the complex was virtually leveled. Only a shell of the fire-blackened tower remained. Three Chinook helicopters were also standing by on the ground for the medical evacuation of badly burned and injured survivors.

As flames began to die down, authorities reported that eight cultists had escaped from the inferno. A short time later one more name was added to the pitifully small list of survivors. Of ninety-four people believed to have been inside the compound, these were apparently the only ones who escaped. Twenty-five of the cultists inside Ranch Apocalypse were seventeen years old or younger.

Four of the survivors were hospitalized with burns or broken bones, two in critical condition. Thirty-year-old Marjorie Thomas, who had fought to reenter the fiery building, was one of the most severely burned. The other critical patient was a seventeen-year-old girl, Misty Ferguson. Her body was charred and bones were broken. She was the youngest of the survivors. Both women were flown to Parkland Hospital in Dallas for treatment in the burn unit.

A couple of men from England were also among the survivors. Thirty-seven-year-old Derek Lovelock, a talented chef with a deep love of the Bible, was recruited by Zilla Henry shortly after breaking up with his wife. Twenty-nine-year-old Renos Avraam also escaped. But his thirty-one-year-old girlfriend, Alison Bernadette Monbelly, who was his partner in a computer business before they left Manchester together for Texas, died in the conflagration.

Others who scrambled out were Clive Doyle, a fifty-two-year-old printer from Australia; Graeme Craddock, a thirty-one-year-old teacher from Australia; twenty-four-year-old Jaime Castillo, a drummer from El Monte, California; thirty-year-old Ruth Ottman, who was also known as Ruth Ellen Riddle; and Balenda Ganem's musician son, David Thibodeaux.

Doctors and nurses at Hillcrest Baptist Medical Center had been on alert throughout the morning, but only one injured cultist was brought there for treatment. Five of the escapees from the compound were taken to the McLennan County Jail in Waco to be held as material witnesses.

None of the men suffered critical burns or other injuries. Koresh, most of his children, several of his wives, and his chief lieutenants all apparently perished in the blaze.

Law enforcement authorities expected it to be days, possibly weeks, before they could give a final accounting of the deaths that occurred in the apocalyptic inferno. A couple of the survivors were initially thought to have escaped the flames by crouching in the tunnels, but government agents couldn't immediately conduct an exhaustive search of the compound because of fears of exploding munitions. Live shells and other munitions continued to explode sporadically throughout much of the afternoon. One explosion occurred more than two days after the fire.

More than one million rounds of unexploded ammunition were found when police at last began moving over the site.

When government officers, investigators from the Texas Rangers, medical examiners, and morticians moved in to begin locating bodies, tagging them for identification and hauling them away, they discovered just what they expected to find. Arms and legs were completely burned off some of the corpses. Many of the remains were reduced to ashes or pitifully charred bones that dissolved into dust when they were touched. There was speculation that the tiny bodies of some of the younger children might have been so completely destroyed by the intense heat that there would be nothing to recover.

Human remains were scattered willy-nilly throughout the compound, individually and in small groups. The largest clump of bodies was found on top of and around the fire-charred concrete bunker built at the base of the watch-tower. Several other corpses were found in a school bus buried in the compound to serve as a bunker.

Federal authorities in Washington reported that on-the-scene observation of skulls and other remains indicated some of the victims may have been shot. The statements led to suspicions some of the cultists had been executed by their companions as they tried to escape. Investigators also had to deal with the possibility, however, that gunshot wounds found on corpses stemmed from the initial shoot-out with the ATF.

Tarrant County Medical Examiner Dr. Nizam Peerwanni brought a team of pathologists from Fort Worth to lead the forensic operation. A man and a woman whose remains were among the first forty bodies removed showed evidence of gunshot wounds.

Dr. Peerwanni said most of the bodies were facedown, indicating death by smoke inhalation. Bodies were photographed, and the locations where they were found were diagramed and marked with small orange flags before removal. As men in combat fatigues began carrying away the remains and placing them in body bags in a nearby tent, they left a ragged field of shattered cement chunks, twisted wire, and bright orange dots listlessly stirring in the breeze. The bodies were eventually transported to Fort Worth, where forensic experts began the grim process of identification and autopsy.

Forensic pathologists were facing an incredibly difficult task because of the severe damage to so many of the bodies. Teeth, especially the back teeth, offered one helpful means of identification if they could be matched with dental records. DNA tests provided another promising method of identification. Commonly referred to as genetic fingerprinting, DNA tests would be carried out by attempting to match the molecular components of blood or other body fluids with those of parents.

As horror stories spread in the wake of the tragedy, there was speculation that adults, to spare the children the fear and pain of dying in the firestorm, may have poisoned them either with lethal injections or pills. No evidence to back up the suspicions was immediately uncovered, however.

The FBI also reported hearing the sound of several gunshots inside the compound at about the time the fire broke out, raising the possibility that cultists attempting to flee might have been murdered.

Even while authorities were poking through the ruins, rumors were already cropping up that the cunningly manipulative cult leader had somehow escaped the fiery holocaust and left his followers behind to die. Another version of Koresh's suspected ability to defeat death was told by a follower who lived outside the compound and predicted his return along with the others who died in the fire. They would be on hand, she assured a reporter, when God set up his heavenly kingdom on earth.

According to government agents, early interviews with at least one of the men who survived backed up the observations of the FBI snipers who reported seeing cultists setting the fires. The FBI reported that the cult member, who found shelter from the flames in the tunnels, said the cultists deliberately doused the interior of the buildings with lantern fuel before setting the fires. A Justice Department spokesman quoted him as saying that as he raced for safety he heard other cultists yelling, "The fire's been lit, the fire's been lit."

Lawyers who talked with the Koreshians, however, reported hearing a different story. They said the survivors blamed the armored assault for starting the blaze. One of the tanks spraying tear gas rammed deep into the building and knocked over a lantern or crushed a barrel of propane, according to the accounts. Flames from the lantern then reportedly ignited hay bales stacked by a window—or set fire to the propane.

Avraam, now being held as a material witness, was taken to a hearing at the federal courthouse in Waco the day after the tragedy when he yelled to reporters: "The fire was not started by us. There were no plans for a mass suicide."

Ricks and other high-ranking law enforcement officials, both at the scene and in Washington, firmly disagreed. Ricks said Koresh wished to kill as many people as possible, including his followers and goverment law enforcment officers.

"His desire, and I stated it repeatedly, as much as I could without seeming overly dramatic, was that he wanted to have as many people killed in that compound as possible," the bureau spokesman told reporters. "That is why it was named the Ranch Apocalypse."

Statements by fire and chemical experts backed up Ricks's remarks blaming the conflagration on the cultists. The pumped-in gas would not have set off the fire, they insisted.

Nevertheless, reverberations from the tragic conclusion to the stalemate set off a flash-fire reaction in Washington, D.C., quickly engulfing the FBI, the Justice and Treasury Departments, and the White House.

"It's a bad end and one of the ends we feared from the beginning," Jack Killorin, an ATF spokesman in Washington, told reporters. "Obviously, suicide was a concern all along, but the method was different, unexpected."

Speaking on NBC-TV, William Sessions said fire wasn't anticipated by planners of the assault. "The setting of fires in the compound brought about a tragedy that none of us expected," the slender, white-haired FBI chief declared. "None of us expected them to commit suicide."

The onetime Waco city councilman also told how concern for the welfare of the children affected the decision to make an attempt to break the stalemate. "There was in fact evidence of the mistreatment of children," he declared. "We know, for instance, from the beginning that some of those children were in fact wives to Mr. Koresh, that there were children who were born to children." There was a systematic pattern of abuse, he said.

But the attorney general took the blame for the tragic resolution to the standoff squarely on her own shoulders. Speaking at a press conference, she declared: "I approved the plan and I'm responsible for it. The buck stops with me."

Ms. Reno was kept busy throughout the day and into the evening, first with the press conference and then with interviews with the print and electronic media. "Obviously, if I had thought that the chances were great for mass suicide, I would never have approved the plan," she said at one point. Another time she observed that "in some instances there are no right answers. I don't think of it as a failure."

She repeatedly cited concern for the welfare of the children as influencing the decision to step up the pressure with tanks and tear gas. She pointed out that Koresh had rejected repeated pleas from negotiators to free the youngsters.

President Clinton appeared to be satisfied to allow his new stand-up Justice Department chief to take the lion's share of the blame for the affair. A brief written statement was released by the White House that had the effect of placing the ultimate responsibility for the decision on her shoulders. "I knew it was going to be done, but the decisions were entirely hers," he said.

By late Monday night she still hadn't heard personally from him, and she publicly conceded they hadn't talked since the tragedy occurred. The president was dining out at a restaurant in Georgetown and touring the new Holocaust Museum while his attorney general took the heat.

Speculation began to drift through Washington and into the press about the possibility of the attorney general resigning. Randall Terry, founder of the antiabortion group Operation Rescue, labeled the affair an example of government terrorism and called for her to step down.

Most talk among government officials and legislators, however, as well as rank-and-file Americans appeared to support her.

There was more public criticism of the president for seeming to dodge responsibility and lay the blame for the disaster on Reno.

Twenty-four hours after the fire, Clinton at last stepped out from behind the attorney general's skirts. He announced during a press conference in the White House Rose Garden that he was calling for an investigation.

This time, after a bit of dodging and weaving, the president publicly accepted full responsibility for the raid. Replying to a question about why he still appeared to be putting the responsibility for the decision on Reno, he said: "Well, what I'm saying is that I didn't have a four- or five-hour detailed briefing from the FBI. I didn't go over every strategic part of it. It is a decision for which I take responsibility. I'm the President of the United States and I signed off on the general decision and giving her the authority to make the last call. . . ."

When he was asked if the attorney general's job was in jeopardy, he came out firmly in her defense. "I was, frankly, surprised would be a mild word, to see that anyone would suggest that the attorney general should resign because some religious fanatics murdered themselves," he declared. A few hours after the president's belated new defense of his attorney general, however, White House spokesmen were already minimizing his role in the decision making.

Neither the statements by the president nor those by the attorney general could lay the matter to rest. Nearly one hundred men, women, and children had died violently since the ATF first attempted to serve the search and arrest warrants almost two months earlier, and people wanted to know whom to blame. The Monday-morning quarterbacking began with a vengeance—on Washington's Capitol Hill; in Austin; and in living rooms, coffee shops, barrooms, and street corners around the nation.

Editorials and columnists questioned the effect the fiasco would have on the new president, asking if it would come to be seen as the most glaring symbol of his leadership failure. Clinton had undergone one political embarrassment after another during his first three months in office, including his attempts to appoint an attorney general acceptable to the legislature.

Plans were announced for a plethora of government and police investigations that promised to keep the tragedy at Ranch Apocalypse in the news for a long time to come, possibly for years.

Arizona Democrat Dennis DeConcini had previously announced that the subcommittee he chairs would hold hearings into the ATF's conduct of the initial raid.

Orrin Hatch of Utah, the senior Republican on the Senate Judiciary Committee, and others called for Senate hearings. Similar demands were made in the U.S. House of Representatives. President Clinton ordered the Treasury Department and the Justice Department to conduct a joint investigation.

As the FBI and ATF began moving out at Ranch Apocalypse, the Texas Rangers were moving in. As the senior investigative agency in the Lone Star State, the Rangers were already conducting their own probe of the disastrous ATF venture, and the even more ghastly resolution to the standoff.

In Waco, Mrs. Ganem disclosed plans to establish a support group to help family members of the cultists deal with their loss—and with the authorities. Waco Mayor J. Robert Sheehy also announced that city agencies would work with family members who had lost relatives in the conflagration. Baptists, Seventh-Day Adventists, Roman Catholics, and other Christians from throughout central Texas gathered in their churches to pray for the dead and for family members left behind to grieve.

Much sorting out of other kinds also remained, including probable criminal trials of some of the cultists and possibly civil trials involving lawsuits against the government. Some survivors of people who had died inside the compound were already firmly convinced they knew who ultimately was at fault. They blamed the ATF, the FBI, and other federal authorities. Before the ashes had cooled at Ranch Apocalypse they were consulting attorneys about lawsuits against the government and claims for damages.

Others who had been involved with the cultists in various ways were convinced that Koresh had planned to lead his followers in mass suicide, regardless of what federal agents may have tried. David Jewell told reporters that his daughter was taught as a young girl that the United States Army would sometime confront the cultists and that Koresh and some of his followers would die in the clash.

If the cultists couldn't lure the military into attacking them, they would press the attack in order to destroy themselves, he said. "They were going to die. Period!"

Jamar, the father of two teenagers, addressed the single aspect of the tragedy that bothered many people the most when he remarked, "Those children are dead because David Koresh had them killed."

Senator Ernest Hollings, a South Carolina Democrat who heads the Senate Appropriations

Committee, which oversees the Justice Department, was quoted in the press with another observation about those who had shot ATF agents. It seemed to sum up the situation for the many observers who felt the FBI had shown great patience and tried its best to avert more bloodshed.

"Fifty-one days was a gracious plenty . . . to apprehend murderers," he said.

**AMY FISHER—VICIOUS KILLER OR VICTIM OF LOVE?**

**THE ELECTRIFYING CASE THAT INSPIRED THE BLOCKBUSTER TV MOVIE!**

While her Long Island high school classmates happily planned dates for the prom, 17-year-old Amy Fisher appalled them with tales of her wild sexual escapades, of her steamy, obsessive alleged affair with a married man— of a wife she wanted out of the picture.

But it wasn't until Amy was arrested for attempting to slay unsuspecting Mary Jo Buttafuoco in cold blood in front of her own home, that police and reporters uncovered Amy Fisher's hidden world—a world that included secret call girl rings, attempts to hire hitmen with payment in sex—and a beeper still nestled in her purse on which clients could page her with personal codes.

# LETHAL LOLITA

## by *Maria Eftimiades*